T0070607

THE PRAYERS
of
KIERKEGAARD

We cannot come to God except through prayer alone, for he is too high above us. MARTIN LUTHER

Prayer is the central phenomenon of religion, the very hearthstone of all piety. FRIEDRICH HEILER

The best help in all action is—to pray, that is true genius; then one never goes wrong.
SOREN KIERKEGAARD

THE PRAYERS
of
KIERKEGAARD

Edited and with a New Interpretation
of His Life and Thought

By
PERRY D. LeFEVRE

THE UNIVERSITY OF CHICAGO PRESS

CHICAGO AND LONDON

The University of Chicago Press, Chicago 60637
The University of Chicago Press, Ltd., London

© 1956 by The University of Chicago
All rights reserved.
Published 1956
Paperback edition 1963
Printed in the United States of America
17 16 15 14 13 12 11 10 09 08   6 7 8 9 10

ISBN-13: 978-0-226-47057-3 (paper)
ISBN-10: 0-226-47057-1 (paper)
LCN: 56-11000

♾ The paper used in this publication meets the
minimum requirements of the American National
Standard for Information Sciences—Permanence of
Paper for Printed Library Materials,
ANSI Z39.48-1992.

PREFACE

One of the most striking phenomena in the intellectual life of the twentieth century has been the rediscovery of the thought of a lonely and tragic figure of the nineteenth century, Soren Kierkegaard. Kierkegaard's influence has been felt in many areas of human thought. Theology, philosophy, psychology, literature, art, and biblical studies have all felt the impact of his mind and spirit. His works have been studied and discussed, understood and misunderstood, from a great variety of perspectives. He has been seen as a poet, as a prophet, as a philosopher, and as a theologian. He has been interpreted by those who were sympathetic and those who were antagonistic, by those who regarded themselves as disciples and by those who thought of themselves as his enemies. His work has been subjected to analysis by Marxists, by psychoanalysts, by Roman Catholics, by orthodox Protestants, and by freethinkers.

The present work does not disparage the possibility or the value of looking at Kierkegaard from any of these viewpoints. It is, however, based on the presupposition that whatever merit other viewpoints may have, Kierkegaard was primarily a religious thinker, a man struggling for his own soul. His central problem was that of becoming a Christian, of realizing personal existence. The key to understanding Kierkegaard lies in his religious writings and in his Journals. His philosophical and aesthetic works are to be understood in the light of his religious works. It has been my intention, therefore, to take the reader to the religious center of Kierkegaard's existence. From this perspective, faith is seen to be Kierkegaard's goal, and *prayer is revealed as man's sole means of moving toward that goal*. This thesis is elaborated through an examination of Kierkegaard's own piety and of his thought on the place of prayer in the life of the Christian. The first part of this work, a collection of Kierkegaard's prayers, has a twofold purpose. It is meant to illuminate the thesis by demonstrating the intimate way in which Kierkegaard's own prayer was fused with his understanding of Christian faith and life. It is also intended to provide a rich resource of devotional material unknown to most contemporary Christians for use in both private and public worship.

Any student of Kierkegaard's life and thought is indebted to a large number of predecessors who have studied and translated the work of this profound thinker. I am aware of my constant obligation to them. I should like also to express publicly my appreciation to my wife for her careful criticism of style and form of expression and to Jens and Harry Thomson, World Church Fellows at the Chicago Theological Seminary in 1954–55 and 1955–56, respectively, for aid in translation of the Danish materials. I owe a further debt of gratitude to the work of P. H. Tisseau, whose little book, *Prières* (Bazoges-en Pareds, 1937), helped me locate many of the prayers and much of the material on prayer within the Danish *Papirer*.

The following publishers have kindly given their permission to make quotations from books to which they hold copyright: the American-Scandinavian Foundation (David F. Swenson's translation, completed and edited by Walter

Lowrie, of Kierkegaard's *Concluding Unscientific Postscript;* David F. Swenson's translation of Kierkegaard's *Philosophical Fragments*); Augsburg Publishing House (David F. Swenson's translation of Kierkegaard's *Thoughts on Crucial Situations in Human Life*, David F. and Lillian Marvin Swenson's translation of Kierkegaard's *The Gospel of Suffering*, David F. and Lillian Marvin Swenson's translation of Kierkegaard's *Edifying Discourses*); Harper and Brothers (Douglas V. Steere's translation of Kierkegaard's *Purity of Heart*); Oxford University Press (Alexander Dru's translation of *The Journals of Soren Kierkegaard*, Walter Lowrie's translation of Kierkegaard's *Christian Discourses*, Walter Lowrie's translation of Kierkegaard's *The Point of View for My Work as an Author*, Walter Lowrie's *Kierkegaard*); Pantheon Books Inc. (Hohlenberg's *Soren Kierkegaard*); Princeton University Press (David F. and Lillian Marvin Swenson's translation of Kierkegaard's *Works of Love*, Walter Lowrie's translations of Kierkegaard's *Training in Christianity*, *Sickness unto Death*, *For Self-Examination*, *The Concept of Dread*, *Repetition*).

PERRY D. LeFEVRE

TABLE OF CONTENTS

PART I
The Prayers

TO THE READER

In the collection of Kierkegaard's prayers which follows I
have placed in the first group those in which Kierkegaard ad-
dresses God the Father; in the second, those addressed to the Son;
and in the third, those addressed to the Holy Spirit. A fourth
group includes prayers for special occasions. I have been guided
in ordering the prayers within each of the groups by Kierkegaard's own principle that true piety emerges from a sense of
one's own unworthiness and of the greatness of God, that it
moves in tension to an understanding of God's love, and then, if
at all, to special petitions. I have titled each prayer either by
using a phrase from the prayer itself or one which seems to
express its central theme. For convenient reference the individual
prayers have been numbered and the source of each prayer may
be found by referring to the pages following the notes to Part II.

My earnest hope is that the reader may find in these prayers
not only an approach to a sensitive and sympathetic understanding of Kierkegaard and his thought but also a rich resource for
his own religious life.

PERRY D. LEFEVRE

I
GOD, THE FATHER

THY GREATNESS, MY NOTHINGNESS

GOD in Heaven, let me really feel my nothingness, not in order to despair over it, but in order to feel the more powerfully the greatness of Thy goodness.

THINE IS THE POWER

FATHER in Heaven! In the external world one is stronger, another is weaker; the first is perhaps proud of his strength and the second perhaps sighs and feels jealous; but in our own inner world we are all weak in the light of Thy countenance, Thou the powerful one, Thou, the only strong one.

THOU ART INCOMPREHENSIBLE

FATHER in Heaven! Thou art incomprehensible in Thy
creation; Thou livest afar off in a light which no one
can penetrate and if we recognize Thee in Thy providence,
our knowledge is feeble and veils Thy splendor, Thou
who art incomprehensible in Thy splendor. But Thou art
still more incomprehensible in Thy grace and in Thy
mercy. What is man that Thou art mindful of him,
Thou Infinite One—but even more, what is the son of
a fallen race, that yea Thou wouldst visit him, Thou Holy
One; yea what is the sinner that Thy Son wouldst come into
the world because of him, not to judge but to save,
not to make known His own dwelling place so that the
lost might seek Him, but in order to seek out that which
is lost, having no den such as wild beasts have, having
no place on which to lay his head, knowing hunger in
the desert, thirst on the Cross. Lord, Father of compassion!
What is man able to do for such great benefits; he is
not even able to give Thee thanks without Thee. Teach
us then the humble discernment of true intelligence that,
as a broken heart sighs under the weight of its guilt,
saying in its sorrow: "It is impossible! it is impossible
that God is able to show such compassion," so that the
one who appropriates this assurance in faith must also
say in his joy, "it is impossible." If death too seemed to
separate those who love one another and again they were
given to each other, their first cry at the moment of

their reunion would be, "it is impossible." And this joyous message of Thy compassion, Father in Heaven, even if man has heard it since his tender infancy, is not for that the less incomprehensible! And even if man meditates on it day by day, it does not become for that less incomprehensible! Was then Thy incomprehensible mercy like that of a man, which disappeared on closer acquaintance, like the happiness of those who loved each other once in days of old incomprehensible (then) but not any more. O torpid human reason! O guileful earthly wisdom! O cold thought of slumbering faith! O miserable forgetfulness of the cold heart! No, Lord, keep Thou everyone who believes in Thee in the proper humble understanding and deliver him from evil.

THOU ART UNCHANGEABLE

O THOU who are unchangeable, whom nothing changes!
Thou who art unchangeable in love, precisely for our
welfare not submitting to any change: may we too will
our welfare, submitting ourselves to the discipline of
Thy unchangeableness, so that we may in unconditional
obedience find our rest and remain at rest in Thy
unchangeableness. Not art Thou like a man; if he is to
preserve only some degree of constancy he must not
permit himself too much to be moved, nor by too many
things. Thou on the contrary art moved, and moved in
infinite love, by all things. Even that which we human
beings call an insignificant trifle, and pass by unmoved,
the need of a sparrow, even this moves Thee; and what
we so often scarcely notice, a human
sigh, this moves Thee, O Infinite Love! But nothing
changes Thee, O Thou who art unchangeable! O Thou
who in infinite love dost submit to be moved, may this
our prayer also move Thee to add Thy blessing, in order
that there may be wrought such a change in him who
prays as to bring him into conformity with Thy
unchangeable will, Thou who are unchangeable!

THY WORD

Father in Heaven, what is man that Thou visitest him,
and the son of man that Thou art mindful of him?—
and in every way, in every respect! Verily, Thou didst
never leave Thyself without a witness; and at last Thou
didst give to man Thy Word. More Thou couldst
not do; to compel him to make use of it, to hear it or
read it, to compel him to act according to it, Thou
couldst not wish. Ah, and yet Thou didst do more. For
Thou art not like a man—rarely does he do anything
for nothing, and if he does, he at least would not be put
to inconvenience by it. Thou, on the contrary, O God,
bestowest Thy Word as a gift—and we men have nothing
to give in return. And if only Thou dost find some
willingness on the part of the single individual, Thou
art prompt to help, and first of all Thou art the one who
with more than human, yea, with divine patience, dost
sit and spell it out with the individual, that he may be
able rightly to understand the Word; and next Thou
art the one who, again with more than human, yea,
with divine patience, dost take him as it were by the
hand and help him when he strives to do accordingly—
Thou our Father in Heaven.

THOU GOD OF LOVE

How could anything rightly be said about love if Thou wert forgotten, Thou God of love, from whom all love comes in heaven and on earth; Thou who didst hold nothing back but didst give everything in love; Thou who art love, so the lover is only what he is through being in Thee! How could anything rightly be said about love if Thou wert forgotten, Thou who didst make manifest what love is, Thou, our Savior and Redeemer, who gave Himself to save us all! How could anything rightly be said about love if Thou wert forgotten, Thou spirit of love, Thou who dost abate nothing of Thine own, but dost call to mind that sacrifice of love, dost remind the believer to love as he is loved, and his neighbor as himself! O eternal love! Thou who art everywhere present, and never without testimony in what may here be said about love, or about works of love. For it is certainly true that there are some acts which the human language particularly and narrow-mindedly calls acts of charity; but in heaven it is certainly true that no act can be pleasing unless it is an act of love: sincere in its self-abnegation, a necessity for love, and just because of this, without claim or merit.

O INFINITE LOVE

Thou loving Father, everything goes wrong for me
and yet Thou art love. I have even failed in holding fast
to this—that Thou art love, and yet Thou art love.
Wherever I turn, the only thing that I cannot do without
is that Thou art love, and that is why, even when I
have not held fast to the faith that Thou art love,
I believe that Thou dost permit through love that it
should be so, O Infinite Love.

8

THOU HAST LOVED US FIRST

FATHER in Heaven! Thou hast loved us first, help us
never to forget that Thou art love so that this sure
conviction might triumph in our hearts over the seduction
of the world, over the inquietude of the soul, over the
anxiety for the future, over the fright of the past, over
the distress of the moment. But grant also that this
conviction might discipline our soul so that our heart
might remain faithful and sincere in the love which we
bear to all those whom Thou hast commanded us to
love as we love ourselves.

THOU WHO HAST FIRST LOVED US

THOU who hast first loved us, O God, alas! We speak
of it in terms of history as if Thou hast only loved us
first but a single time, rather than that without ceasing
Thou hast loved us first many times and everyday and
our whole life through. When we wake up in the
morning and turn our soul toward Thee—Thou art
the first—Thou hast loved us first; if I rise at dawn and
at the same second turn my soul toward Thee in prayer,
Thou art there ahead of me, Thou hast loved me first.
When I withdraw from the distractions of the day and
turn my soul in thought toward Thee, Thou art the
first and thus forever. And yet we always speak
ungratefully as if Thou hast loved us first only once.

THOU HEAREST OUR CRY

FATHER in Heaven! Great is Thine infinite kingdom.
Thou who bearest the weight of the stars and who
governest the forces of the world through immense
spaces; numberless as the sands are those who have life
and being through Thee. And yet, Thou hearest the cry
of all the creatures, and the cry of man whom Thou
hast specially formed. Thou hearest the cry of all men
without confusing their mixed voices and without
distinguishing one from another in such a way as to play
favorites. Thou hearest not only the voice of one who
is responsible for many others and so prays to Thee in
their name, as if his high function could bring him nearer
to Thee; Thou hearest not only the voice of one who
prays for dear ones, as if he could thereby attract Thine
attention, he who is privileged in having the dear ones;
no, Thou hearest also the most miserable, the most
abandoned, and most solitary man—in the desert, in the
multitude. And if the forgotten one has separated himself
from all others; and if in the crowd he has become
unknown—having ceased to be a man except as a number
on a list—Thou knowest him. Thou has not forgotten
him. Thou rememberest his name; Thou knowest him
where he is, retired, hidden in the desert, unperceived
in the crowd, in the multitude. And if in the thick
shadows of dread, in the prey of terrible thoughts, he
was abandoned by men, abandoned almost by the

language men speak, still Thou wouldst not have forgotten him. Thou wouldst understand his language. Thou knowest also how quickly to find a way which leads to him, quick as sound, prompt as light; and if Thou shouldst wait it is not slowness, but wisdom; and if Thou dost wait, it is not slowness, but because Thou only knowest the speed of Thy help; if Thou dost wait, it is not stingy parsimony, but paternal economy which keepest the best things reserved for the child, in a secure place, for a favorable moment. Lord our Father! Man cries to Thee in the day of distress and he gives thanks to Thee in the day of joy. Oh how wonderful to give thanks when man understands so easily that Thou art the giver of good and perfect gifts, when even the earthly heart is at once ready to understand and when even earthly prudence speedily consents. More blessed though it is to give thanks when life becomes a darkened story; more blessed though to give thanks when the heart is oppressed and the soul darkened, when reason is a traitor in its ambiguity and memory is mistaken in its forgetting, when egoism recoils in fright, when human wisdom resists, if not in rebellion then in discouragement—more blessed then to thank God, for the one who thus is thankful truly loves God. He dares to say to Thee, Thou all knowing God: Lord, Thou knowest all things, Thou knowest I love Thee.

11

THY LOVING CARE

FATHER in Heaven! In the evening, when we prepare
to go to sleep, we are consoled by the thought that Thou
art the one who watches over us—and yet, when we
awaken in the morning and when we remain awake
during the day, what a desolation if Thou wert not the
one watching over us! The difference that we establish
between sleep and waking is then only a pleasantry—
as if we needed Thy wakefulness only as long as we are
asleep, but not when we ourselves are awake.

THY FATHERLY CARE

FATHER in Heaven! Thou who dost care for the sparrow
without cruelly requiring that he be like Thee, no,
Thou who dost concern Thyself for the sparrow in this
way, Thou dost put Thyself in his place in Thy fatherly
solicitude. Yea, also Thou dost so concern Thyself with
man. If Thou requirest of him that he try to resemble
Thee, an effort which Thou art not able to require of
the sparrow, Thou dost not, however, require it cruelly.
No, in Thy fatherly solicitude, Thou dost put Thyself
in his place, and Thou art Thyself the one who givest
him the strength for the task.

HAVE THEN A LITTLE PATIENCE

FATHER in Heaven! Show unto us a little patience; for we often intend in all sincerity to commune with Thee and yet we speak in such a foolish fashion. Sometimes, when we judge that what has come to us is good, we do not have enough words to thank Thee; just as a mistaken child is thankful for having gotten his own way. Sometimes things go so badly that we call upon Thee; we even complain and cry unto Thee; just as an unreasoning child fears what would do him good. Oh, but if we are so childish how far from being true children of Thine who art our true Father, ah, as if an animal would pretend to have man as a father. How childish we are and how little our proposals and our language resemble the language which we ought to use with Thee, we understand at least that it ought not to be thus and that we ought to be otherwise. Have then a little patience with us.

LET US NOT FORGET

AND if Thou dost permit us to know the many
magnificent secrets of science, do not let us forget the
one thing necessary; and if Thou dost desire to extinguish
our vigor of mind or if Thou dost let us grow old on
earth so that our soul gets weary, one thing there is that
can never be forgotten, even if we forget all else, that
we are saved by Thy son.

HOLD NOT OUR SINS

FATHER in Heaven! Hold not our sins up against us but hold us up against our sins, so that the thought of Thee when it wakens in our soul, and each time it wakens, should not remind us of what we have committed but of what Thou didst forgive, not of how we went astray but of how Thou didst save us!

SEEKING THEE IN THE CONFESSION OF SINS

FATHER in Heaven! We know indeed that seeking is
never without its promise, how then could we fail to
seek Thee, the author of all promises, and the giver of all
good gifts! We know well that the seeker does not
always have to wander far afield, since the more sacred
the object of his search the nearer it is to him; and if he
seeks Thee, O God, Thou art of all things most near!
But we know also that that seeking is never without its
pains and its temptation, how then would there not be fear
in seeking Thee, who art mighty! Even he who trusts
in thought to his kinship with Thee, does not venture
forth without fear upon those crucial decisions of thought,
where through doubt he seeks to trace Thy presence in
the wise order of existence, or through despair he seeks
to trace Thee in the obedience under providence of
rebellious events. He, whom Thou dost call Thy friend,
who walks in the light of Thy countenance, he, too,
not without trembling, seeks the meeting of friendship
with Thee, who alone art mighty. The man of prayer
who loves with his whole heart—it is not without anxiety
that he ventures into the conflict of prayer with his God.
The dying man, for whom Thou dost shift the scene,
does not relinquish the temporal without a shudder
when Thou dost call him. Not even the child of woe,

for whom the world has nothing but suffering, flees to
Thee without fear, Thou who dost not merely alleviate,
but art all in all! How then should the sinner dare to
seek Thee, O God of righteousness! But therefore he
seeks Thee, not as these others do, but he seeks Thee in
the confession of sins.

AGAINST YOU HAVE I SINNED

O GOD, you have nothing but trouble with us men!
Alas, when at the thought of all your kind actions to me
I try to collect my thoughts in order to thank you
properly—alas, I often find myself so distracted, the most
varied thoughts rush through my head and it all ends
with my praying to you to help me to thank you—yet
this much a benefactor might ask, not to be caused still
further trouble by being asked to help one to thank him!

Oh, and when for a moment sin gains power over me
in new sin—then when my soul is inconsolable I do not
know what to do but say to you: You must help me,
you must console me, find something in which I can find
consolation, so that my sin may even explain itself by
helping me further than I should otherwise have come.
How unashamed—It is you against whom I have sinned,
and then to ask you to console me for it.

And yet I know that this does not displease your infinite
love, for that is, in a sense, a sign of progress! If sin
has complete power over a man, then he dare not think
of you at all; if he fights against it, but not with all his
strength, then at the most he only dares accuse himself
before you and beg your forgiveness. But if he fights

with all his strength, honestly—then only can it occur to him that you are in such a way party with him, or on his side, that it is you who will console him, that instead of merely accusing himself before you he almost dares to complain, as though it were something which had happened to him.

THOU ART ABLE TO HEAL

FATHER in Heaven! To Thee the congregation often makes its petition for all who are sick and sorrowful, and when someone amongst us lies ill, alas, of mortal sickness the congregation sometimes desires a special petition; grant that we may each one of us become in good time aware what sickness it is which is the sickness unto death, and aware that we are all of us suffering from this sickness. O Lord Jesus Christ, who didst come to earth to heal them that suffer from this sickness, from which, alas, we all suffer, but from which Thou art able to heal only those who are conscious that they are sick in this way; help Thou us in this sickness to hold fast to Thee, to the end that we may be healed of it. O God the Holy Ghost, who comest to help us in this sickness if we honestly desire to be healed; remain with us so that for no single instant we may to our own destruction shun the Physician, but may remain with Him—delivered from sickness. For to be with Him is to be delivered from our sickness, and when we are with Him we are saved from all sickness.

FATHER in Heaven! Open Thou the wells of our eyes like a flood, let tears wash out our past life which did not find grace before Thine eyes; but give us also a sign as of old, as when Thou didst set a rainbow like a portal of grace in the heavens, that Thou wilt not obliterate us with a flood; never let sin gain such power in us that Thou needest again to drive us out of the *body* of sin.

THE SUPREME DANGER

O GOD, there are in the outside world so many things
which would turn us from Thee; that is why we enter
into Thy house, but even here there is sometimes a
misleading security, as if all danger and all terror were
far away, here, where even the supreme danger is to be
confronted: that of sin, and the supreme terror: the
passion and the death of Christ.

THY FORGIVENESS

GOD of Love! Thou hast commanded us to forgive our enemies, our brother in error, not seven times, but seventy times seven: When then wilt Thou tire of pardoning a truly repentant sinner?

22

WE BELONG TO THEE

FATHER in Heaven! Draw our hearts to Thee, that our
heart may be where our treasure must be, that our
thoughts may aspire to Thy kingdom where our
citizenship is so that our departure when Thou shalt
call us may not be a painful separation from this world
but a blissful reunion with Thee. Still we do not know
the time or the season; perhaps it is still far from us.
But when at times our strength is taken from us, when
lassitude overcomes us like a kind of fog in which our
vision is plunged as into a dark night, when our desires,
our impatience, and our anger are stirred up, when our
hearts tremble in anxiety awaiting what is to come, then,
O Lord our God, teach us and strengthen this conviction
in our hearts, that also in this life we belong to Thee.
Amen.

TO WILL ONE THING

FATHER in Heaven! What is a man without Thee!
What is all that he knows, vast accumulation though
it be, but a chipped fragment if he does not know Thee!
What is all his striving, could it ever encompass a world,
but a half-finished work if he does not know Thee:
Thee the One, who art one thing and who art all!
So may Thou give to the intellect, wisdom to comprehend
that one thing; to the heart, sincerity to receive this
understanding; to the will, purity that wills only one
thing. In prosperity may Thou grant perseverance to will
one thing; amid distractions, collectedness to will one
thing; in suffering, patience to will one thing. Oh, Thou
that givest both the beginning and the completion,
may Thou early, at the dawn of day, give to the young
man the resolution to will one thing. As the day wanes,
may Thou give to the old man a renewed remembrance
of his first resolution, that the first may be like the last,
the last like the first, in possession of a life that has willed
only one thing. Alas, but this has indeed not come to
pass. Something has come in between. The separation of
sin lies in between. Each day, and day after day something
is being placed in between: delay, blockage, interruption,
delusion, corruption. So in this time of repentance may
Thou give the courage once again to will one thing.
True, it is an interruption of our ordinary tasks; we do
lay down our work as though it were a day of rest,

when the penitent (and it is only in a time of repentance
that the heavy-laden worker may be quiet in the
confession of sin) is alone before Thee in self-accusation.
This is indeed an interruption. But it is an interruption
that searches back into its very beginnings that it might
bind up anew that which sin has separated, that in its
grief it might atone for lost time, that in its anxiety it
might bring to completion that which lies before it.
Oh, Thou that givest both the beginning and the
completion, give Thou victory in the day of need so
that what neither a man's burning wish nor his determined
resolution may attain to, may be granted unto him in
the sorrowing of repentance: to will only one thing.

THAT I MAY BELIEVE

Father in Heaven, when I consider the matter of my
eternal happiness, then I do not bring out the reckoning;
for I know, indeed, that I cannot answer one to a
thousand, and I also know that Peter stood more securely
upon the waves of the sea, than does the one who stands
on his own unrighteousness against Thee. And I will
not build my eternal happiness on any deed I may have
done, not even the best, for only Thou dost know
whether it was a good deed; and not upon the best that
I might do, for only Thou dost know whether it might
become a good deed. Preserve, then, my soul from the
pettiness that would disparage Thee and Thy gift.
disparage myself by making myself greater than others.
Preserve my soul from the reflection which would
penetrate what is not given me to understand. Tear out
from my soul the sophistry which cunningly takes the
best and leaves me the poorer. What as a child I did
easily and naturally, in that I believed without understanding;
what I have done later, have done, I know, have believed
a man against reason; what I shall continue to do,
even if being clever is commended more highly than
believing; what I shall strive to do with all my might,
so that the glory of the intellect shall not deceive me and
injure my soul: should I not be willing to do it for Thee;
should I not, since I can still do nothing of myself, wish
for concern and confidence and sincerity in believing
Thee, and in this faith expect Thy eternal happiness.

COMMITTED TO THEE
and so at last be saved

THEREFORE, will we commit to Thee, Father in Heaven,
our heart and our thought, so that our soul may never
be so ensnared by the joys of life or by its sorrows,
that it forgets this liberating word; but so that it may
not too often be impatience and inner disquiet which
bring this word to our lips; so that when, like a faithful
friend, it has accompanied us through all the many
relations of life, has accommodated itself to us, yet
without being false to itself, has been our consolation,
our hope, our gladness, our cause of rejoicing; has sounded
to us solemnly and inspiringly, softly and soothingly;
has spoken to us warningly and admonishingly, cheerfully
and invitingly; that then our soul in its last hour may
be carried away from the world on this word, as it were,
to that place where we shall understand its full
significance. So we may understand that the same
God who by His hand led us through the world, now
withdraws it and opens His embrace to receive the
longing soul. Amen.

THAT WE MAY BE FAITHFUL

THOU who in our earliest childhood hast received our promise, Thou to whom at baptism we gave our promise of faithfulness, Father in Heaven, grant that throughout our life we do not forget our promise, our engagement, that we do not forget to come to Thy wedding, whatever excuses we might find, these pretexts are indifferent things; the decisive thing for us would be that we didn't come to the wedding.

27

FOR FAITH

TEACH me, O God, not to torture myself, not to make a martyr out of myself through stifling reflection, but rather teach me to breathe deeply in faith.

TO KNOW THY WILL

FATHER in Heaven! Reawaken conscience in our breast.
Make us bend the ear of the spirit to Thy voice, so that
we may perceive Thy will for us in its clear purity as it
is in Heaven, pure of our false worldly wisdom, unstifled
by the voice of passion; keep us vigilant so that we may
work for our salvation with fear and trembling; oh,
but grant also that when the Law speaks most strongly,
when its seriousness fills us with dread, when the thunder
booms from Sinai—Oh grant that we may hear also a
gentle voice murmuring to us that we are Thy children,
so that we will cry with joy, Abba, Father.

AT THY COMMAND

GOD give me strength to think only of what I have to do;
show me Thy will and command me to act as Thou
didst once upon a time command the prophet Elijah:
if you meet a man upon the road do not greet him, and
if he greet you, do not greet him in return.

NOT LIKE STRANGERS

HEAVENLY Father! Teach us to walk before Thy face and grant that our thoughts and our acts may not be like strangers coming from afar for a rare visit to Thy dwelling place but rather like native sons they might perceive that Thou livest in us. Of what use would it be if such a visit were full of splendor? Of what use would it be if our face shone like that of Moses when he spoke to the Eternal? Of what use would it be to hide our face as Moses did before the Jews in order to mask the rapid disappearance of that radiance? Let us never forget that Christianity is a whole course of life, so that even though I stood at the outer boundaries of Thy Kingdom, O Holy Father, far away by myself like the toll collector of old, if only I stood there facing Thee—and did not turn again like the one who puts his hand to the plow—staff in hand ready to travel, and even though mountains, valleys, and rivers lay before my feet, yet I have the promise: the smallest in the Kingdom of Heaven is greater than what is born of women.

FOR COURAGE

My lord God, give me once more the courage to hope; merciful God, let me hope once again, fructify my barren and infertile mind.

LET ME NOT BE DISCOURAGED

FATHER in Heaven! As a father sends his son out into the world, so also hast Thou sent man down here; he is, it seems, separated from Thee by a world; he does not see Thee with his eyes; he does not hear Thy voice with his ears of flesh. He stands now in the world, the way opens before him—so long weakened in the discouraging moment which will not give him time, so impassive in the moment of enervating impatience which will not give him time; give then to Thy child freedom from discouragement in the vast world, freedom from discouragement when false leads seem so numerous and the right road so difficult to find. Give him the freedom from discouragement when dread and care seem to be undergirded by the destructive furor of the elements and the terror of events and by the despair of human misery; give then to Thy child the courage to remember and believe that as a father sends his child into the world, Thou hast also sent man down here. God of compassion! As the prodigal son found everything changed on his return, even the disposition of his brother, but not that of his father whose fatherly love he received and who welcomed with a festival, whose fatherly love gave him courage in his discouragement at the festival. Even so, when a man turns back toward Thee, Thou givest him courage on his road to conversion, for his return is not joyous like that of the well-loved child returning home, but it is painful like that of the prodigal son, and he is not thus expected by a loving father who with joy awaits his loving son and is joyous at seeing him again. Ah, that he may have courage to believe that a compassionate Father, who in His solicitude dreads his perdition, is awaiting him.

33

FOR THY PEACE

O LORD, calm the waves of this heart; calm its tempests!
Calm thyself, O my soul, so that the divine can act
in thee! Calm thyself, O my soul, so that God is able
to repose in thee, so that His peace may cover thee!
Yes, Father in Heaven, often have we found that the
world cannot give us peace, O but make us feel that
Thou art able to give peace; let us know the truth of
Thy promise: that the whole world may not be able to
take away Thy peace.

FOR PEACE AND ASSURANCE

To THEE, O God, we turn for peace . . . but grant us too
the blessed assurance that nothing shall deprive us of
that peace, neither ourselves, nor our foolish, earthly
desires, nor my wild longings, nor the anxious cravings
of my heart.

35
FROM THE LILIES AND THE BIRDS
LET US LEARN
Be not anxious for your life. . . . MATT. 6

FATHER in Heaven, when spring is come, everything in
nature returns in new freshness and beauty, the lilies
and the birds have lost nothing of their charm—oh,
that we also might return to the instruction of these
teachers! Ah, but if in the time that has elapsed we have
lost our health, would that we might regain it by learning
again from the lilies of the field and the birds of the air!

THAT WE MIGHT LEARN

FATHER in Heaven! What one in society with men, especially there in the human swarm, with so much difficulty learns to know, and what, in case one has elsewhere learned to know it, is so easily forgotten in society with men, namely, what it is to be man, and what in a godly understanding of it is the requirement for being man—oh, that we might learn this, or, if it is forgotten, that we again might learn it from the lilies and the birds; that we might learn it, if not all at once and all in all, yet at least something of it, and little by little; that at this time we might from the lilies and the birds learn silence, obedience, joy!

GUIDES FOR THE TROUBLED

FATHER in Heaven! From Thee come only good and perfect gifts! Those whom Thou dost appoint to human beings for teachers, to the troubled for guides, their teaching and their guidance it must also be beneficial to follow. So grant us, then, that the troubled may in truth learn from those divinely appointed teachers: the lilies of the field and the birds of the air! Amen.

THE THOUGHT OF THEE

FATHER in Heaven! When the thought of Thee wakes in our hearts let it not awaken like a frightened bird that flies about in dismay, but like a child waking from its sleep with a heavenly smile.

I WILL CONTINUE TO PRAY

AND when at times, O Lord, Thou seemest not to hear my voice, my plaint, my sigh, my thanksgiving, I will even then continue to pray to Thee until Thou hearest my thanksgiving because Thou hast heard me!

HELP US TO PRAY

GRANT that our prayer be not like the flower which today is and tomorrow is cast into the oven, not like the flower even though in magnificence it surpasses the glory of Solomon.

LOVE OF THEE MAKETH ELOQUENT

AND if one says that earthly love makes one eloquent,
how much greater reason, O Lord, for saying that the
love one bears for Thee will make men eloquent, Thou
who hast Thyself formed the mouth of man for the word.

FOR SELF-MASTERY

Lᴏʀᴅ! Make our heart Thy temple in which Thou wouldst
live. Grant that every impure thought, every earthly
desire might be like the idol Dagon—each morning
broken at the feet of the Ark of the Covenant. Teach us
to master flesh and blood and let this mastery of ourselves
be our bloody sacrifice in order that we might be able
to say with the Apostle: "I die every day."

BE NEAR TO US

Our Father, be near to us with Thy power so that we may feel a joyous assurance of heart that Thou art not far from us, but that we live and move and have our being in Thee.

WE WOULD TURN TOWARD THEE

FATHER in Heaven! We would turn our soul and our thoughts toward Thee for Thou art the one who lifts up and casts down. Though we are honored in the world; though we are responsible for important things among men, our effort, our conduct, our aspiration, our hope in this world have not found acceptance before Thine eyes, Thou just God: Oh what then is such human glory compared with this misery! Though cast down, annihilated, misunderstood, abandoned—alone with our care in this world—yet, Thy glance sees in secret and is delighted to question us about our effort, our conduct, our desire, our hope in this world. Oh what then are these adversities as compared with this happiness! Humiliated and broken by the thought of our fault; strangers before men through our sins with no word of consolation; yet our repentance has found a way to Thy throne, Thou merciful God, and has found grace in Thine ears. Oh what then are these sufferings as compared with this happiness! Yes, Lord, we would turn our thoughts and our soul toward Thy will, for Thou art the one who raises up and casts down— toward Thee, our Father which art in Heaven.

WE SEEK THEE AT THIS HOUR

FATHER in Heaven! Our thought is turned toward Thee; again it seeks Thee at this hour, not with the unsteady step of a lost traveler but with the sure flight of a bird homeward bound. Grant then that our confidence in Thee be not a fugitive thought, a momentary leap, a mistaken appeasement of the heart and flesh. Grant that our aspirations toward Thy Kingdom, our hopes for Thy glory, be not unproductive birth pangs or waterless clouds, but that from the fulness of our heart they will rise toward Thee, and that being heard they will quench our thirst like the refreshing dew and satisfy us forever like Thy heavenly manna.

OUR DEPENDENCE ON THEE

FATHER in Heaven! Go Thou with us as Thou hast walked with the Jews in the days of old. Oh, let us not believe that we have outgrown Thine education, but let us grow in it, grow under it, as the good seed groweth in patience. Let us not forget what Thou hast done for us, and when Thy helping hand hath wondrously been there, then let us not seek it again as ungrateful beings who only ate and were satisfied. Grant us to feel that without Thee we can do nothing—a feeling not of cowardly dependence but a feeling of hopeful strength, in the happy assurance that Thou art powerful among the weak.

DRAW NEAR TO ME, O GOD

FATHER in Heaven! Avert Thy countenance from me no longer, let it once again shine upon me so that I may walk in Thy path, and not lose myself further and further away from Thee, where Thy voice can no longer reach me. O, let Thy voice come unto me, be heard by me even though it overtake me with terror on the wrong path, where I live secluded and alone, as though sick and besmirched, far from communion with Thee and mankind. Thou, my Lord Jesus Christ, Thou who camest into the world in order to save those who were lost, Thou who didst leave the ninety and nine sheep in order to look for the lost one, look Thou for me in the path of my errors, where I hide myself from Thee and from mankind, Thou the good shepherd let me hear Thy gentle voice, let me know it, let me follow it! Thou Holy Spirit, come before me with inexpressible sighs, pray for me as Abraham prayed for depraved Sodom, if there be only one pure thought, only one better feeling in me, that the time of trial may be prolonged for the barren tree, O Holy Spirit, Thou who dost bear again those who are already dead, who dost give youth to the old, renew my heart and create in me a new heart, Thou who with motherly care dost protect everything in which there is still a spark of life. O also preserve me bound ever faster to Thee my Saviour, my Redeemer, that I may not, when cured, forget, like the nine lepers, to return to Him who has given me life, in whom alone blessedness is found; bless my action and my thought, so that it may be known that I am His serf now and in all eternity.

LET US FEEL THY PRESENCE

THOU who art in all places, when I meditate on what I will say and how I will say it, Thou art present; when the individual has resolved to come into Thy house, Thou art present, but perhaps the thought is not truly present to him: Bless then this worship in order that each one of us individually will in this hour feel Thy presence and know that we are before Thee.

THOU ART NEAR

FATHER in Heaven! Well do we know that Thou art everywhere present; and that should anyone at this moment call upon Thee from his bed of sickness, or one in greater need upon the ocean cry out to Thee, or one in still greater need in sin, that Thou art near to hear him. But Thou art also near in Thy house where Thy community is gathered together, some perhaps flying from heavy thoughts, or followed by heavy thoughts, but some too coming from a quiet daily life of contentment, and some perhaps with a satisfied longing hidden in a thankful heart enveloped in joyous thoughts—and yet all drawn by the desire to seek God, the friend of the thankful in blessed trust; consolation of the weak in strengthening communion; refuge of the anxious in secret comfort; confidante of the afflicted as Thou dost count their tears; last comfort of the dying as Thou dost receive their souls. So let Thyself be found also in this hour; Thou who art the Father of all, let Thyself be found with a good gift for everyone who needs it, that the happy may find courage to rejoice at Thy good gifts, that the sorrowful may find courage to accept Thy perfect gifts. For to men there is a difference in these things, the difference of joy and of sorrow, but for Thee, O Lord, there is no difference in these things; everything that comes from Thee is a good and perfect gift.

THY LOVE IS BEYOND ALL PROOF

THERE was a time, O God, when Thou hast heaped upon me precious gifts, and for a benefit received I thought of Thee. This was happiness. Then all has changed; it seemed to me that I succeeded in nothing, and each time a new misfortune came, I thought of Thee. I thought that Thou art love: This happiness was still greater. For Thy love is not like man's love that must be proved by his acts toward Thee. Oh no, Thy love is beyond all proof: Whatever Thou doest to Thy subject it is infinite love. And when has there been greater truth in me than when I felt that Thou art infinite love? It was certainly not when I had proof, Oh no, it was when I felt it without proof, when it was not a dogma, which always needs demonstration, but had for me become an axiom which never needs such, Oh, but when my soul becomes weary, then Thou dost not leave me without proof.

A GOODNESS GREATER THAN THE HUMAN
HEART CAN UNDERSTAND

FATHER in Heaven! Thou dost hold all good gifts in Thy
gentle hand. Thy abundance is richer than human
understanding can apprehend. Thou art more willing to
give and Thy goodness is greater than the human heart
can understand. Thou dost fulfil every prayer and dost
give what we pray for, or that which is far better than the
thing for which we ask. So dost Thou give everyone his
appointed share, as it is pleasing to Thee. But, too, Thou
dost give everyone the assurance that all things come from
Thee, that no joy can separate us from Thee in the
forgetfulness of pleasure, no sorrow effect a separation
between Thee and us; but that we may resort to Thee in
our gladness, and abide with Thee in our sorrow, so that
when at last our days are numbered, and the outward
man has perished, death may not come in his own name,
cold and terrible, but gentle and friendly, with greetings
and messages, with testimony from Thee, Our Father
Who Art in Heaven! Amen.

EVERY GOOD AND PERFECT GIFT

Every good and every perfect gift is from above and cometh down from the Father of lights, with whom is no variableness nor shadow of turning. These words are so beautiful, so eloquent, so moving; they are so soothing and so comforting, so simple and comprehensible, so refreshing and so healing.

THEREFORE we will beseech Thee, O God, that Thou wilt make the ears of those who hitherto have not regarded them, willing to accept them; that Thou wilt heal the misunderstanding heart by the understanding of the word, to understand the word; that Thou wilt incline the erring thought under the saving obedience of the word; that Thou wilt give the penitent soul confidence to dare to understand the word; and that Thou wilt make those who have understood it more and more blessed therein, so that they may repeatedly understand it. Amen.

ALL THINGS WORK TOGETHER FOR GOOD
TO THEM THAT LOVE THEE

EVERY time that I have understood Thy goodness toward
me I have thanked Thee before mankind for all Thy
blessings; oh, but that is not really the relation between
Thee and man—that he is able to understand that Thou
art good. Help me to thank Thee even then when I do
not understand that Thou art good but almost like a child
want to believe that Thou art less loving. Abominable
thought, by which I could make myself eternally unhappy.

Often though it seems to me that my relation to Thee is
like that which I might have to an examiner: It is necessary
that I use my reason, my strength; and then it is a question
of knowing if I have grasped the truth. If I am mistaken
Thou dost say simply: "Yes, here you are mistaken"; or
"You have done wrong—you have yourself to blame."
O my God, is this the relation between God and a man!
No, God be praised, Thou and I—we are not face to face
in such a noble equality. Oh no, even when I am mistaken,
Thy providence has been there, permitted my mistake,
and in its love has made my error enter into Thy paternal
designs for me, disposing in Thy love these millions of
possibilities in such a way that even my error has in truth
been profitable to me.

Thou hast made me succeed in everything; then came a
time when it seemed to me that Thou didst make me fail
in everything. Then I thought all was over, that Thou

wouldst have nothing more to do with me. Then I came to think that there would still be one blissful thing left for me: to thank Thee without ceasing for the unspeakable good that Thou hast done for me, in a measure infinitely greater that I had expected. Oh the littleness of my heart which in all things has thought of Thee in such a small way. No, Thine intention was that I should advance through this unspeakable blessing Thou hast given me, that I should know the joy of praising Thee and giving Thee thanks even when I cannot understand and when everything seems to be going against me.

WHATEVER COMES OF THEE

Father in Heaven! Let us consider that whatever happens to us, this comes from Thee, and that of whatever comes from Thee nothing is able to harm us; no, no, it can only be to our benefit.

55
WE WOULD RECEIVE ALL

WE WOULD receive all at Thy hand. If it should be honor and glory, we would receive them at Thy hand; if it should be ridicule and insults, we would receive them at Thy hand. Oh let us be able to receive either the one or the other of these things with equal joy and gratitude; there is little difference between them, and for us there would be no difference if we thought only of the one decisive thing: that it comes from Thee.

NOT EMPTY-HANDED

GOD of compassion! We know that every good gift and ever perfect gift cometh down from Thee, but Thou hast not sent us into the world empty-handed: grant that our hand might not be closed, our heart not hardened but add Thou Thyself the blessing so that our gift might come from on high, from Thee, good and perfect.

EVERY CREATURE TURNS ITS EYES
TO THEE

LORD our God! Every creature turns its eyes to Thee and
awaits its nourishment and its subsistence from Thee.
Thou openest Thy compassionate hand and Thou dost fill
abundantly with blessing all who live. Thou hearest the
cry of the beast; Thou listenest to the complaint of man.
And those to whom Thou hast given much raise their
thoughts to Thee, for they know that all cometh from
Thee and that no abundance satisfies if Thou dost not bless
it; and in the same way, those to whom thou hast given
little, for they know that no gift cometh from Thee which
is so small that with Thy benediction it is not superabundant.

IT IS FROM THY HAND

FATHER in Heaven! It is from Thy hand that we receive
all. Thou stretchest forth Thy powerful hand and it
seizes the wise in their foolishness; Thou stretchest forth
Thy powerful hand and worlds pass away. Thou openest
Thy compassionate hand and it fills with abundant blessing
all that live, and if at times Thou seemest to take Thy
hand from us, we know that Thou dost only close it in
order to conceal a blessing yet more abundant. We know
that Thou dost only close Thy hand in order to open it
again and to fill abundantly with blessing all who live.

ALL THINGS COME OF THEE

O LORD, our relation to Thee is not like one which we
might have with a man from whom we buy—it is first
necessary for Thee to give and only then can one speak
about our duty of buying from Thee what Thou hast
given: faith, hope, charity, good aspirations, a favorable
season. Thou givest everything and for nothing, without
receiving any payment (for only the pagan who did not
know Thee thought that the gods did not give something
for nothing). But when Thou hast given Thou requirest
that we buy from Thee what Thou hast given. Thus
Thou dost humble Thyself to walk among us in our
humanity and Thou art not ashamed of being our God,
and yet toward Thee we act as we might toward a child;
in giving him something, we pretend in order to give
him pleasure that he himself will give us what we
have given to him and what belongs to us. (And our
relation with God is not even of this kind, for God is both
the one who gives and the one who makes it possible for
us to give. The situation would then be like that in which
a father or a mother helps a child write an anniversary
letter which the parent would later himself receive as a gift.)

60

GIVE US THE STRENGTH

Lord our God, Thou knowest our sorrow better than
we know it ourselves. Thou knowest how easily our
fearful soul entangles itself with untimely and self-made
cares. We pray Thee: Let us clearly discern their
inappropriateness and scorn them proudly, these busy
self-made cares. But whatever care Thou dost inflict upon
us, let us receive it from Thy hand with humility and give
us the strength to bear it.

THINE INFINITE WISDOM

O MY God, how often have I not rejoiced, given thanks, been unspeakably grateful in discovering how wondrously events have been ordered; that I would do sc·nething and only later I would fully understand that the course of events was significant and just. But at times also I have had to say with overflowing joy: "My God, Thy wisdom disposes—in making use of my stupidity." I do not fail to act with considered judgment, but I still do some stupid or imprudent things, and I am at the point of losing courage, thinking that now even everything is lost, and then afterward I understand that exactly this stupidity Thou has turned into infinite wisdom. Infinite love!

ONE THING WILL REMAIN

OH, IF everybody were against me, and if one misfortune
followed another (which often causes more pain than does
human opposition which you know must come), one
thing, however, will remain, O God, the testimony of
the Spirit. When Thou, who dost order all things and
who at each moment confrontest millions of possibilities,
when Thou who art infinite love, dost let everything get
in my way, or I have brought this about through my own
errors; when then Thou who art infinite love dost permit
me to make mistakes and dost seem to retire, there is yet
between us a community—the testimony of the Spirit.
Without it, that is, if by this means Thou didst not hold
fast even the one whom Thou dost test most severely,
I would be at my wits' end—it would be impossible to
know where I was, if the reverses are Thy paternal
reprimand destined to make me recoil with fright, or if
these difficult times do not signify exactly that I am on the
right road, the narrow road to which the witness of the
Spirit is the only signpost.

THOU DOST NOT LOVE ME
FOR MY MERITS

DEEP down in my soul Thou hast planted the happy
assurance that Thou art love. Thou hast treated me
paternally like a child; teaching me the same thing a second
time, Thou hast shown me that Thou art love. Then Thou
hast kept Thy silence for a moment; Thou hast wished to
try me on my own without proof to see if I would come
to the same conclusion all alone. Then have I seen
everything confounded; I have been filled with dread and
fear even to the point of imagining that this task was too
much for me, afraid that I had gone too far, had become
too familiar with Thee, or had tried Thy patience too
long, and that I was being punished. Relieve me from one
burden alone, I said: that this might not be held against
me. . . . Miserable ingrate that I was; as if it was because
of my wisdom and my merits that Thou didst love me
before, O, heart full of folly and vanity which wants to
gain something by lies for itself from the past and is not
content with having experienced the bliss that God is love
and that He proves it to you, but still wants to persuade
itself that it has to some extent been worthy of this love,
if only compared to its present unworthiness. Oh no, no,
God be praised, it has never been on account of my
merits that God has loved me. It is exactly this which
gives me true courage. If not, then man must at this
instant die of dread in the thought that in the next instant
he may be less worthy.

THY SILENCE

FATHER in Heaven! Thou dost speak to man in many ways;
Thou to whom alone belongeth wisdom and understanding
yet desirest Thyself to be understood by man. Even when
Thou are silent, still Thou speakest to him, for the one
who saith nothing, yet speaketh in order to examine the
disciple; the one who saith nothing, yet speaketh in order
to try the beloved one; the one who saith nothing, yet
speaketh so that the hour of understanding may be more
profound. Is it not thus, Father in Heaven! Oh, in the
time of silence when man remains alone, abandoned when
he does not hear Thy voice, it seems to him doubtless
that the separation must last forever. Oh, in the time of
silence when a man consumes himself in the desert in
which he does not hear Thy voice, it seems to him
doubtless that it is completely extinguished. Father in
Heaven! It is only a moment of silence in an intimacy of
conversation. Bless then this silence as Thy word to man;
grant that he never forgets that Thou speakest also when
Thou art silent; give him this consolation if he waits on
Thee, that Thou art silent through love and that Thou
speakest through love, so that in Thy silence as in Thy
word Thou art still the same Father and that it is still the
same paternal love that Thou guidest by Thy voice and
that Thou dost instruct by Thy silence.

THE JOY IN SUFFERING

O MY God, my God, unhappy and tormented was my childhood, full of torments my youth. I have lamented, I have sighed, and I have wept. Yet I thank Thee, not as the wise Sovereign; no, no, I thank Thee, the one who art infinite love, for having acted thus! Man has before him a life of thirty, forty, perhaps seventy years; in Thy love Thou hast prevented me from buying for this sum just the little sweets of the kind for which I would have no memory in eternity, or which I would even recall for my eternal torment—as having bought the worthless.

Thou hast obliged me (and there were also many moments in which Thou hast spoken with kindness but of the same thing, not that I should escape the suffering but that it was even Thy love which placed me in these sufferings). Thou hast obliged me to buy these sufferings: blessed. For each suffering thus bought is the communion in suffering with Thee, and is forever and forever an eternal acquisition, for one remembers only one's suffering.

66

KEEP ME FROM BECOMING A FOOL

KEEP me from becoming a fool who will not accept Thy chastisement, or a rebellious fool who is unwilling to accept Thy chastisement, a fool who is unwilling to accept it for his blessing, or a rebellious fool who wants to accept it for his perdition.

67

THANKS. BE TO GOD

How I thank you, Father in Heaven, that you have
preserved my earthly father here upon earth for a time
such as this when I so greatly need him, a father who, as
I hope, will with your help have greater joy in being my
father the second time than he had the first time in being so.

2
GOD, THE SON

Whither should we turn, if not to Thee, Lord Jesus Christ? Where might the sufferer find consolation, if not in Thee? Ah, and where the penitent, if not with Thee, Lord Jesus Christ?

TO WHOM CAN WE TURN?

LORD Jesus Christ, though indeed Thou didst not come into the world to judge the world, yet as love which was not loved Thou wast a judgment upon the world. We call ourselves Christians, we say that we have none to turn to but to Thee—alas, where might we go when to us also, just because of Thy love, the condemnation applies that we love little? To whom (oh, disconsolate thought!) if not to Thee? To whom then (oh, counsel of despair!) if Thou really wouldst not receive us mercifully, forgiving us our great sin against Thee and against love, forgiving us who have sinned much because we loved little?

THOU ART OUR ONLY HIDING PLACE

O LORD Jesus Christ, the birds have their nests, the foxes their holes, and Thou didst not have whereon to lay Thy head, homeless wert Thou upon earth, and yet a hiding-place, the only one, where a sinner could flee. And so today Thou art still the hiding-place; when the sinner flees to Thee, hides himself in Thee, is hidden in Thee— then he is eternally defended, then "love" hides a multitude of sins.

DRAW US TO THEE

Yea, Lord Jesus Christ, whether we be far off or near, far away from Thee in the human swarm, in business, in earthly cares, in temporal joys, in merely human highness, or far from all this, forsaken, unappreciated, in lowliness, and with this the nearer to Thee, do Thou draw us, draw us entirely to Thyself.

THERE IS SO MUCH TO DRAG US BACK

O LORD Jesus Christ, there is so much to drag us back:
empty pursuit, trivial pleasures, unworthy cares. There
is so much to frighten us away: a pride too cowardly to
submit to being helped, cowardly apprehensiveness which
evades danger to its own destruction, anguish for sin
which shuns holy cleansing as disease shuns medicine.
But Thou art stronger than these, so draw Thou us now
more strongly to Thee. We call Thee our Saviour and
Redeemer, since Thou didst come to earth to redeem us
from the servitude under which we were bound or had
bound ourselves, to save the lost. This is Thy work,
which Thou didst complete, and which Thou wilt
continue to complete unto the end of the world; for since
Thou Thyself hast said it, therefore Thou wilt do it—
lifted up from the earth Thou wilt draw all unto Thee.

73

WEAK IS OUR FOOLISH HEART

O LORD Jesus Christ, weak is our foolish heart, and only too ready to let itself be drawn—and there is so much that would draw it to itself. There is pleasure with its seducing power, the manifold with its confusing distractions, the moment with its deceptive importance, and bustle with its vain toil, and frivolity's careless squandering of time, and melancholy's gloomy brooding— all of these would draw us away from our own self and to them, in order to deceive us. But Thou who art the truth, only Thou our Saviour and Redeemer, canst truly draw a man to Thee, which indeed Thou hast promised to do, to draw all unto Thyself. So God grant that we by entering into ourselves may come to ourselves, so that Thou, according to Thy word, canst draw us to Thee—from on high, but through lowliness and humiliation.

74

UNTO THEE IN LOWLINESS

O LORD Jesus Christ, many and various are the things to
which a man may feel himself drawn, but one thing
there is to which no man ever felt himself drawn in any
way, that is, to suffering and humiliation. This we men
think we ought to shun as far as possible, and in any case
that we must be compelled to it. But Thou, our Saviour
and Redeemer, Thou who wast humbled yet without
compulsion, and least of all compelled to that humiliation
in the imitation of which man discovers his highest honor;
ah, that the picture of Thee in thy humiliation might be
so vivid to us that we might feel ourselves drawn unto
Thee in lowliness, unto Thee who from on high wilt
draw all unto Thyself.

THY LIFE IS THE JUDGMENT

O LORD Jesus Christ, Thou who indeed didst not come to judge, but wilt come again to judge the world. Thy life on earth is in reality the judgment by which we shall be judged. Wherefore everyone who calls himself a Christian must test his life by this judgment, to discern whether he loves Thee in Thy humiliation, or loves Thee only in Thine exaltation, or simply whether he loves Thee, for if it is only in one of these two ways he loves Thee, he loves Thee not. But if he loves Thee, he surely shall experience humiliation (for he loves Thee in Thy humiliation), but not as when the worldly mind succumbs to humiliation—for it was not thus Thou didst walk here on earth in humiliation. No, such a lover, though humiliated, is raised above humiliation, his mind, his eye, being directed to the high places wherein Thou hast entered, and where he looks forward to being with Thee who from on high wilt draw all unto Thyself.

THOU ART THE STRONGEST

LORD Jesus Christ, there are so many things to keep us
and to draw us to themselves; each one of us has his
own particular attraction, yet all of us have many. But
Thine attraction is eternally the strongest! Draw us then
the more powerfully to Thee. We call Thee our Redeemer
for Thou art come into the world to break our bondage
to the vain cares which we have imposed upon ourselves,
to break the heavy chains of sin. We call Thee our Saviour
that Thou mightest save us by freeing us from all these
fetters. For it is God's will that Thou shouldst accomplish
this and make possible our sanctification. That is why
Thou hast descended into the lower regions of the earth
and that is why Thou hast returned to Heaven in order
to draw us to Thine own dwelling place.

HELP US TO LOVE THEE

LORD Jesus Christ, that we may be able rightly to pray
Thee for all things, we pray first for one: help us to love
Thee much, increase love and inflame it. Oh, this is a
prayer Thou wilt surely hear, Thou who indeed art not
love of such a sort—so cruel a sort—that Thou art only
only the object, indifferent to whether any one loves Thee
or not; Thou indeed art not love of such a sort—in wrath—
that Thou art only judgment, jealous of who loves Thee
and who does not. Oh, no, such Thou art not; Thou
wouldst thus only inspire fear and dread, it would then
be terrible "to come to Thee," frightful "to abide with
Thee," and Thou wouldst not be the perfect love which
casteth out fear. No, compassionate, or loving, or in love,
Thou art love of such a sort that Thou Thyself dost woo
forth the love which loves Thee, dost foster it to love
Thee much.

Thou alone, O Lord, art able to move a man; from the moment that I think of Thee, my life is at Thy service; my weak talents are perhaps great in the eyes of men, but for Thee they are nothing and in every case they are the gifts Thou hast given me. When I think of Thy sufferings, Thou, my Lord and Saviour, I do not want to spend my days whimpering in a pulpit, but I want to be surrounded by insults, losing everything which is of earthly order—if it is Thy will.

THOU who didst come into the world in order to suffer,
and who hast borne the heaviest of all sufferings,
intensified still more in the heaviest of all pain, the
measure in which it was freely accepted: the suffering of
knowing in advance, from the first moment of Thy life,
Thy constant power of avoiding it; Thou who hast
suffered all Thy life and finally suffered an ignominious
death, thanks be to Thee for having sanctified suffering,
for having by Thy life and by Thy holy actions clarified
for our happiness the meaning of that suffering which
remains for natural man an eternal darkness. Thanks be
to Thee, that the man who suffers shall never forget the
great blessing which consoles and abundantly strengthens
and brings the heavenly light of its explanation, but may
he not have the presumption to forget the difference
which gives humility, to forget that Thou hast suffered
innocently for the guilty, or to forget this difference,
which still consoles beyond all measure, that Thy death
was our redemption.

A WHOLE LIFE LONG

LORD Jesus Christ! A whole life long didst Thou suffer that I too might be saved; and yet Thy suffering is not at an end; but this too wilt Thou endure, saving and redeeming me, this patient suffering of having to do with me, I who so often go astray from the right path, or even when I remained on the straight path stumbled along it or crept so slowly along the right path. Infinite patience, suffering of infinite patience. How many times have I not been impatient, wished to give up and forsake everything, wished to take the terribly easy way out, despair; but Thou didst not lose patience. Oh, I cannot say what Thy chosen servant says: that he made up what was lacking in the afflictions of Christ in his flesh;* no, I can only say that I increased Thy sufferings, added new ones to those which Thou didst once suffer in order to save me.

* Col. 1:24.

NOT TO ADMIRE BUT TO FOLLOW

O LORD Jesus Christ, Thou didst not come to the world to be served, but also surely not to be admired or in that sense to be worshipped. Thou wast the way and the truth—and it was followers only Thou didst demand. Arouse us therefore if we have dozed away into this delusion, save us from the error of wishing to admire Thee instead of being willing to follow Thee and to resemble Thee.

WOULD THAT WE MIGHT FOLLOW THEE

O LORD Jesus Christ, who didst behold Thy fate in
advance and yet didst not draw back; Thou who didst
suffer Thyself to be born in poverty and lowliness, and
thereafter in poverty and lowliness didst bear the sin of
the world, being ever a sufferer, until, hated, forsaken,
mocked, and spat upon, in the end deserted even by God,
Thou didst bow Thy head in the death of shame—oh,
but Thou didst yet lift it up again, Thou eternal victor,
Thou who wast not, it is true, victorious over Thine
enemies in this life, but in death wast victorious even
over death; Thou didst lift up Thy head, forever victorious,
Thou who art ascended to heaven! Would that we might
follow Thee!

PATTERN AND REDEEMER

O LORD Jesus Christ, it was not to plague us men but to
save us that Thou didst say, "No man can serve two
masters"—oh, that we might be willing to accept it, by
doing it, that is, by following Thee! Help us all and
everyone, Thou who art both willing and able to help,
Thou who art both the Pattern and the Redeemer, and
again both the Redeemer and the Pattern, so that when
the striver sinks under the Pattern, then the Redeemer
raises him up again, but at the same instant Thou art the
Pattern, to keep him continually striving. Thou, our
Redeemer, by Thy blessed suffering and death, hast made
satisfaction for all and for everything; no eternal blessedness
can be or shall be earned by desert—it has been deserved.
Yet Thou didst leave behind Thee the trace of Thy
footsteps, Thou the holy pattern of the human race and
of each individual in it, so that, saved by Thy redemption,
they might every instant have confidence and boldness
to will to strive to follow Thee.

THINE EXAMPLE

THOU, who didst once wander on earth, leaving footprints which we should follow; Thou, who still from Thy heaven dost look down upon each wanderer, dost strengthen the weary, encourage the despondent, lead back the erring, comfort the striving; Thou who also at the end of days shalt return to judge whether each man individually has followed Thee: our God and our Saviour, let Thine example stand clearly before the eyes of our soul to disperse the mists; strengthen us that unfalteringly we may keep this before our eyes; that we by resembling and following Thee may later find the way to the judgment, for it behooves every man to be brought to the judgment, oh, but also through Thee to be brought to eternal happiness hereafter with Thee. Amen.

HELP ME TO THINK OF THEE

O LORD Jesus Christ, so permeate my thought that it
could be seen that I am thinking of Thee. And how
would one see it? Would it be in my glance turned
toward the heavens? That might also mean that I was
looking at stars, or at visions, or at chimeras. No, if Thine
example gave me such a conviction that though scorned
and mocked I proclaimed Thy doctrine, then one would
see in me (not in my glance but in my daily life) that
I was thinking of Thee.

And you celestial Powers, you who undergird the good,
you heavenly host, help me raise my voice so that
if possible it may be heard throughout the whole world—
I have only one word to say, but if the power were
given me to say that single word, that single phrase
in such a fashion that it would remain fixed and
unforgettable—my choice is made; I know what I would
say: "Our Lord Jesus Christ was nothing, oh, remember
this, Christendom."

THY CHURCH MILITANT

O LORD Jesus Christ, doubtless it is from on high Thou dost draw a man to Thyself, and it is to victory Thou dost call him, but this is to say that Thou dost call upon him to strive and dost promise him victory in the strife whereunto Thou dost call him, O Thou mighty Victor. So then preserve us, we pray Thee, as from all other errors, so also from this, that we might imagine we are members of a Church already triumphant here in the world. Thy kingdom indeed was not of this world and is not; this world is not the abode of Thy Church, there is only room for it if it will strive and by striving make room for itself to exist in. But if it will strive, it shall never be driven out of the world, that Thou dost vouch for. On the other hand, if it imagines that it is to triumph here in the world, then, alas, it is itself to blame for that Thou didst withdraw Thy support, then it has perished, then it has confounded itself with the world. Be then with Thy militant Church, that it may never come to pass (in the only way in which it could come to pass) that it should be blotted out from the earth by becoming a triumphant Church.

3
GOD, THE HOLY SPIRIT

ENLIGHTEN OUR MINDS

LORD Jesus Christ, let Thy Holy Spirit enlighten our minds and convince us thoroughly of our sin, so that, humbled and with downcast eyes, we may recognize that we stand far, far off and with a sigh, "God be merciful to me a sinner"; but then let it befall us by Thy grace as it befell that publican who went up to the Temple to pray and went down to his house justified.

THOU SPIRIT OF HOLINESS

WE HAVE our treasure in earthen vessels, but Thou,
O Holy Spirit, when Thou livest in a man, Thou livest
in what is infinitely lower. Thou Spirit of Holiness, Thou
livest in the midst of impurity and corruption; Thou
Spirit of Wisdom, Thou livest in the midst of folly; Thou
Spirit of Truth, Thou livest in one who is himself deluded.
Oh, continue to dwell there, Thou who dost not seek a
desirable dwelling place, for Thou wouldst seek there in
vain, Thou Creator and Redeemer, make a dwelling for
Thyself; oh, continue to dwell there, that one day Thou
mightest finally be pleased by the dwelling which Thou
didst Thyself prepare in my heart, foolish, deceiving,
and impure as it is.

89

BLESS THIS OUR GATHERING

THOU Holy Ghost, Thou makest alive, bless also this
our gathering, the speaker and the hearer; fresh from the
heart it shall come, by Thine aid, do Thou let it also go
to the heart.

SEND THEREFORE THY SPIRIT

Be ye therefore Sober (I Pet. 4:7).

FATHER in Heaven, Thou art a spirit, and they that
worship Thee must worship Thee in spirit and in truth—
but how in spirit and in truth if we are not sober, even
if we are striving to be? Send therefore Thy Spirit into
our hearts; ah, it is so often invoked that it may come to
bring courage, and life, and power, and strength, oh, that
it first (this is indeed the condition for all the rest, and
that the rest may be to our profit), oh, that first it might
make us sober!

O HOLY SPIRIT

O HOLY Spirit—we pray for ourselves and for all—O, Holy Spirit, Thou who dost make alive; here it is not talents we stand in need of, nor culture, nor shrewdness, rather there is here too much of all that; but what we need is that Thou take away the power of mastery and give us life. True it is that a man experiences a shudder like that of death when Thou, to become a power in him, dost take the power from him—oh, but if even animal creatures understand at a subsequent moment how well it is for them that the royal coachman took the reins, which in the first instance prompted them to shudder, and against which their mind rebelled—should not then a man be able promptly to understand what a benefaction it is towards a man that Thou takest away the power and givest life?

4
FOR SPECIAL OCCASIONS

THE NEW YEAR

ANOTHER year has passed, O Heavenly Father! We thank
Thee that it was a time of grace, and we are not terrified
by the thought that it was also a time for which we shall
render an account; for we trust in Thy mercy. The New
Year confronts us with its demands; and though we
cannot enter upon it without humility and concern,
because we cannot and will not forget the lusts of the
eye that ensnared us, the sweets of revenge that seduced
us, the wrath that made us irreconcilable, the coldness of
heart in which we fled from Thee, yet we do not enter it
altogether empty-handed. For we take with us the
memory of fearful doubts which were set at rest, of
anxieties which were solaced, of the downcast mind which
was cheered and strengthened, of the glad hope which
was not put to shame. Aye, and when in our melancholy
moods we seek strength and encouragement in the
thought of the great men, Thy chosen instruments, who
in sharp trials and profound anxieties kept their souls free,
their courage unbroken, the heavens open above them,
then we also wish to add to theirs our testimony,
convinced that even if our courage is but discouragement
in comparison with theirs, and our strength weakness,
nevertheless, Thou art ever the same, the same mighty
God who tires the spirits of men in combat, the same
Father without whose knowledge no sparrow falls to the
ground. Amen.

AT THE LORD'S TABLE

FATHER in Heaven, well we know that it is Thou that
givest both to will and to do, that also longing when it
leads us to renew the fellowship with our Saviour and
Redeemer is from Thee. But when longing lays hold of
us, oh, that we might lay hold of the longing; when it
would carry us away, that we might give ourselves up;
when Thou art near to summon us, that we also might
keep near to Thee in supplication; when Thou in the
longing dost offer us the highest good, that we might
buy the opportune moment, might hold it fast, sanctify
it in a quiet hour with serious thoughts, with pious
resolutions, so that it might become the strong but also
well-tested longing which is required of them that would
worthily partake of the Holy Communion! Father in
Heaven, longing is Thy gift; no one can bestow it upon
himself, when it is not given no one can buy it though
he were willing to sell all—but when Thou givest it, then
one can sell all to buy it. So we pray for them that are
assembled here, that with hearty longing they may today
approach the Lord's Table, and that when they go hence
they may go with increased longing for Him, our Saviour
and Redeemer.

AT THE LORD'S TABLE

FATHER in Heaven! As on other occasions the intercession
of the congregation is that Thou wouldst comfort all
them that are sick and sorrowful, so now at this hour its
intercession is that to them that labor and are heavy
laden Thou wouldst give rest for their souls. Oh, and
yet this is hardly an intercession. Who might count
himself so sound that he need only pray for others? Ah,
no, every one prays on his own account that Thou
wouldst give him rest for his soul. O God, to each one
severally whom Thou beholdest laboring and heavy laden
with the consciousness of sin, do Thou give rest for his
soul.

FATHER in Heaven, Thy grace and mercy change not with
the changing times, they grow not older with the course
of years, as if, like a man, Thou wert more gracious one
day than another, more gracious at first than at the last;
Thy grace remains unchanged, as Thou art unchangeable,
it is ever the same, eternally young, new every day—for
every day Thou sayest, "yet today." Oh, but when one
gives heed to this word, is impressed by it, and with a
serious, holy resolution says to himself, "yet today,"
then for him this means that this very day he desires to
be changed, desires that this very day might become
important to him above all other days, important because
of renewed confirmation in the good he once chose, or
perhaps even because of his first choosing the good. It is
an expression of Thy grace and mercy that every day
Thou dost say, "yet today," but it would be to forfeit
Thy grace and mercy and the season of grace if a man
were to say unchangeably from day to day, "yet today";
for it is Thou that bestowest the season of grace "yet
today," but it is man that must grasp the season of grace
"yet today." Thus it is we talk with Thee, O God;
between us there is a difference of language, and yet we
strive to make ourselves understood of Thee, and Thou
dost not blush to be called our God. That word which
when Thou, O God, dost utter it is the eternal expression
of Thy unchangeable grace, that same word when a man

repeats it with due understanding is the strongest expression of the deepest change and decision—yea, as if all were lost if this change and decision did not come to pass "yet today." So do Thou grant to them that today are here assembled, to them that without external prompting, and hence the more inwardly, have resolved "yet today" to seek reconciliation with Thee by the confession of their sins, to them do Thou grant that this day may be truly blessed to them, that they may hear His voice whom Thou didst send to the world, the voice of the Good Shepherd, that He may know them, and that they may follow Him.

AT THE LORD'S TABLE

Remind me, Jesu, yet again
Of all Thine anguish and distress,
Remind me of Thy soul's deep pain.
                    (Lines of a familiar Danish hymn)

Aʜ, ɪᴛ is true, our Lord and Saviour, that not even in
this respect dare we rely upon our own strength, as
though we were able of ourselves to recall impressively
enough and to retain steadily this remembrance of Thee,
we who would so much rather dwell upon the joyful side
than upon the sorrowful, we who all of us desire for
ourselves good days and the peace and security of happy
times, we who prefer to remain unaware in a profounder
sense of the dreadful things, lest, as we foolishly think,
they might make our happy life gloomy and serious, or
indeed Thine unhappy life, as we are prone to regard it,
all too gloomy and serious. Hence we pray Thee, since
it is Thee we are now to remember, that Thou wouldst
Thyself remind us of these things. Oh, it is a strange
language a man talks when it is with Thee he has to talk;
it is as though it had become unserviceable when it has to
express our relationship to Thee or Thine to us. What is
that for a remembrance when he who is to be remembered
must himself remind the rememberer! Humanly, it is
only the man highly exalted and mighty, with so many
and such important things to think about, who says to the
lowly man, "You must yourself remind me to remember

you." Ah, and it is this very thing we say to Thee, Thou Saviour and Redeemer of the world! Ah, and this same thing when we say it to Thee is precisely the expression of our lowliness and nothingness in comparison with Thee who art with God exalted above all heavens! We pray that Thou Thyself wilt remind us of Thy suffering and death, wilt remind us again and again, in our labor, in our joy, and in our sorrow, of the night in which Thou wast betrayed. For this we make supplication, and we give Thee thanks when Thou dost remind us, and now we thank Thee in behalf of them who are here assembled to approach Thine altar in order to renew their fellowship with Thee.

AT THE LORD'S TABLE

O LORD Jesus Christ, who didst first love us, who until
the end didst love them whom Thou didst love from
the beginning, who unto the end of days dost continue
to love him who would belong to Thee; Thy faithfulness
cannot deny itself—oh, only when a man denies Thee
can he compel Thee as it were to deny him also, Thou
loving One. So be this our comfort when we must accuse
ourselves of the offences we have committed and of the
things we have left undone, of our weakness in temptation,
of our slow progress in the good, in short, of our
unfaithfulness to Thee, to whom once in early youth
and ofttimes again we promised faithfulness—this be our
comfort, that even if we are unfaithful, Thou dost remain
faithful, Thou canst not deny Thyself.

GREAT art Thou, O God; though it is in a dark saying we
know Thee and as in a mirror, yet we adore Thy
greatness with wonder—how much more must we one
day extol it when we learn to know it more fully! When
I stand under the dome of heaven, surrounded by the
marvels of creation, I extol Thy greatness with a heart
deeply stirred to adoration for Thee who dost easily
support the stars in infinite space and with fatherly care
dost concern Thyself with the sparrow. But when we are
assembled here in Thy holy house we are everywhere
surrounded with that which in a deeper sense reminds us
of Thy greatness. For great art Thou, the Creator and
Sustainer of the world; but when Thou, O God, didst
forgive the sin of the world and didst reconcile Thyself
with the fallen race, ah, then Thou wast still greater in
Thine inconceivable compassion! How could we then
but with faith render unto Thee praise and thanksgiving
and adoration in Thy holy house where everything
reminds us of this, and reminds especially those who
today are assembled to receive the forgiveness of sins and
to appropriate to themselves anew the reconciliation with
Thee in Jesus Christ?

AT THE LORD'S TABLE

THOU who didst come down from heaven to bring a blessing to the fallen race; Thou who didst wander here upon earth, unappreciated, betrayed, mocked, condemned— but blessing; Thou who in the act of blessing wast parted from Thine own as Thou didst ascend again into heaven, Thou our Saviour and Redeemer, bless also to them that today are here assembled their participation in the holy Supper in remembrance of Thee. Oh, if at every meal something is wanting in case the blessing is lacking, what then might be this holy meal of grace without Thy blessing? It would not even exist, for it is indeed the supper of blessing!

PART II

*An Interpretation of Kierkegaard's
Life and Thought*

Chapter 1

HIS LIFE

The outward life of Soren Kierkegaard can be quickly told. He was born May 5, 1813, the last of seven children of the second marriage of Michael Pedersen Kierkegaard; he lived nearly all his life in Copenhagen. Spared the necessity of earning his own living by his father's wealth, he was in turn a university student, a serious author, and finally a polemical writer. He entered the university in 1830 and took his Master's degree in 1841. He became engaged to Regine Olsen in 1840, and the engagement was broken a little more than a year later. From 1843 until his death in 1855 he published a large number of aesthetic, philosophical, religious, and polemical works, many of them pseudonymously.* Frequently seen in the streets talking to ordinary folk, or at the theater, or conversing with his friends in the cafés, he was a well-known figure in Copenhagen both among the common people and in intellectual and religious circles. Even as a young man he was famous for his brilliance and wit. Later he was subjected to ridicule and notoriety at the hands of a comic paper, the *Corsair*, which he had assailed for scandal-mongering. Toward the end of his life he became a controversial figure because of his prophetic attack on the mediocrity and pretension of the bourgeois Christianity of his time. Kierkegaard died, well known but hardly understood or appreciated, on November 18, 1855.

This simple story of the events of his outward life is deceptive; it veils the interminable complexity and depth of his inwardness. The real story of Kierkegaard's life is the history of the inner movement of mind and spirit. Because of the complexity of his authorship, his deliberate mystification, and his inability to reveal himself (*Indesluttethed*), this story cannot be fully grasped from his published works and was unknown to his contemporaries. With the publication of his personal papers a part of his story has become known, but, as he predicted, his deepest secret lies buried with him, and all attempts to wrest it from him seem to have failed.[1] Some indication of the complexity of his life is to be found in the conflicting pictures of this man disclosed in contemporary evidences and in his own Journals. That the same complexity characterized his authorship is well illustrated in his own view of the pseudonymous writings.

In his youth, according to Nielsen the headmaster of his preparatory school, Kierkegaard was gay, open, and innocent. As he looks back on his own childhood, Kierkegaard makes us aware that something very different was going on inside him than appeared to the external observer:

From a child I was in the power of a monstrously brooding temperament, the depth of which found its only true expression in the equally monstrous dexterity given to me, of concealing it under an outward appearance of joviality and vivacity. My sole joy, from practically as far back as I can remember, was that no one could possibly discover how unhappy I was.[2]

Some interpreters have held that Kierkegaard has in retrospect overemphasized the melancholy of his childhood and that this accounts sufficiently for the incongruity of the two impressions. Be this as it may, the same incongruity continued into later life as is evidenced by a comparison of the descriptions of those who knew him on intimate personal terms with the introspective meditations of his Journals. Thus his niece, Henriette Lund, writes of her Uncle Soren's visits with her family as if he were the most cheerful of men —an ideal companion for children. She characterizes him as "a great tease"; he had "a hidden affection and tenderness" about him; he was "full of jokes and fun"; his laughter was contagious. When Kierkegaard's father died, she reports that, so far as the observer could see, he treated the whole thing as a bagatelle. Many years afterward when the first volume of the *Papirer* appeared, she reports her Uncle Christian's remark: "Yes, what an uncomfortable thought, that a man who always looked so cheerful should have been so fundamentally melancholy. . . ."[3] From the *Papirer* we too can see the terrible and pervasive melancholy which characterized his inner life all through this time, and we can know how deeply he was affected by the death of his father.

The same point is to be made with reference to his authorship, for as he makes clear in his comment on the pseudonymous works at the end of the *Concluding Unscientific Postscript* there is in these works "not a single word which is mine."[4] He has poetically produced these authors, and their work is to be regarded as their own production, not his. On the other hand, though he is literally to be taken as the author of the *Edifying Discourses,* even these works are not to be taken as a full revelation of Kierkegaard's own thinking or of the depths of his religious life. Only as he moves in his later years toward greater and greater openness does the complexity of his authorship begin to resolve itself into simplicity. Both his life and his work are examples of his own principles: that the inner is not the outer; that everyone is finally impenetrable; and that the depths of personal existence cannot be fully grasped in the realm of the objective.

Since the publication of his *Papirer*, however, it has become possible to reconstruct at least something of Kierkegaard's personal struggle and to understand something of the intimate relationship between his life and thought. Kierkegaard has been much written about as a poet, as a philosopher, as a prophet in relation to his age. In a sense he was all of these, but more than any of these and underlying them all he can be seen now as a religious man struggling for his own soul. Seen in this perspective, he should not finally be judged as either poet, or philosopher, or prophet, but he should rather be sympathetically understood in the context of his own pilgrim's progress. It may even be true, as Heidegger suggests, that Kierkegaard's fruitfulness for philosophy rests more in the religious character of his writing than in any contribution he may have made to philosophy as such.[5]

KIERKEGAARD'S SENSE OF VOCATION

One of the ways of approaching an understanding of Kierkegaard's inner life is to see his struggle as the development of a sense of personal vocation. That this problem of vocation was a significant one for him, even in his early youth, can be seen in the following excerpt from a letter which he addressed to his sister's brother-in-law, Peter Lund, in 1835:

Everybody would like their work in the world to be according to the measure of their abilities in a particular direction, in that which is most suited to their individuality. But what is that? That is where I stand, like Hercules, but not at the parting of the ways—no, here there is a far greater number of ways and it is correspondingly difficult to choose the right one. The misfortune of my life is perhaps that I am interested in far too many things and not decidedly in some one thing; my interests are not all subordinated to one thing but are all co-ordinated.

And yet

Life has interested me most in virtue of reason and freedom, and to elucidate and solve the riddle of life has always been my desire.[6]

A few months later he writes in his Journal of what might be called his problem of vocation in a deeper sense:

What I really lack is to be clear in my mind *what I am to do,* not what I am to know, except in so far as a certain understanding must precede every action. The thing is to understand myself, to see what God really wishes *me* to do; the thing is to find a truth which is true *for me,* to find the *idea for which I can live and die.* What would be the use of discovering so-called objective truth, of working through all the systems of philosophy and of being able, if required, to review them all and show up the inconsistencies within each system;—what good would it do me to be able to develop a theory of the state and combine all the details into a single whole, and so construct a world in which I did not live, but only held up to the view of others;—what good would it do me to be able to explain the meaning of Christianity if it had *no* deeper significance *for me and for my life;* what good would it do me if truth stood before me, cold and naked, not caring whether I recognized her or not, and producing in me a shudder of fear rather than a trusting devotion? I certainly do not deny that I still recognize an *imperative of understanding* and that through it one can work upon men, *but it must be taken up into my life*, and *that is* what I now recognize as the most important thing.[7]

In a sense Kierkegaard's whole life and thought can be understood as his attempt to come to terms with the questions he poses in the preceding entry. This was the continuing problem of his life and thought. To be sure, in the richness of his thought, Kierkegaard expresses the same idea in many different ways: He is seeking to know himself, for "one must know one's self before knowing anything else";[8] and knowing himself comes to mean finding himself and being himself. These in turn come to mean finally being found by God. Or Kierkegaard is searching for the Archimedean point from which he can lift the whole world; this he comes to find first in fatherly love and then finally in prayer alone before God.[9] Or he is seeking personal truth, for "what is truth but to live for an idea?"[10] However we depict the goal and direction which shaped Kierkegaard's life and thought, the ultimate answer to his quest came in terms of Christianity. The idea turns out to be Christ; integrity is seeking the Kingdom first; the Archimedean point is prayer alone before the Christian God; the meaning of life is to be found in becoming a Christian. To trace the development of Kierkegaard's sense of vocation is to trace his deepening understanding of the relationship of his life and his work to the Christian faith.

Kierkegaard's earliest relation to the Christian faith was by his own admission ambivalent. He was both filled with dread by Christianity and yet attracted to it. He had had a strict Christian upbringing by a father whose prayer for his son was: "Be sure that you really love Jesus Christ."[11] Encouraged by his father and following in his brother Peter's footsteps, he became a candidate in theology at the University of Copenhagen. During his extended university career he continued to wrestle with the problem of his own relation to the Christian faith. It was a time of moving away from both his father and his father's faith. It was a time of inner turmoil, of a rebellion against his father which he later came to understand as a rebellion against God himself. Theological study seems neither to have appealed to him nor to have helped him. Orthodoxy, rationalism, Schleiermacher, the Grundtvig movement—all failed to speak to his inner need. In his studies he was chiefly concerned with aesthetics and philosophy. Apart from his studies he appeared to be something of a dilettante, yet beneath the surface of his busyness and lack of serious concern he sensed the aimlessness and emptiness of his own life. His experience and reflection carried him further and further toward disillusionment and despair. What was happening to him after 1835 can be symbolized by his great interest in the legends of Faust, Don Juan, and the Wandering Jew. The problems of skepticism and doubt, sensuality and despair, were those which most concerned him. Not only had he failed to resolve his ambivalence to the Christian faith through theological study but he had also moved away from any positive relationship to the faith. He still maintained an intellectual interest in Christianity, but even here he was critical. In his Journal he wrote that as soon as he began to think for himself the huge colossus of orthodox dogma started to totter for him. Though Christianity had become less of an option for him, it still remained in his thought as a "radical cure," but this cure he would forego. Christianity was an offense to his reason and to his feeling. Kierkegaard speculated about the relation of Christianity to philosophy and concluded that the two were irreconcilable.[12] He thought that Christianity set the faithful at odds with the world, and he himself was worldly; he saw that Christianity demanded conversion, a leap of despair, and such a leap was not for him, at least in 1835.[13]

Little by little, however, as life became a bitter drink for him, as his own deep melancholy was woven into his reflections on despair, guilt, and sin, he became less and less confident that philosophy was the answer to his quest for meaning. The ambiguity of his own life, the compounding of his own sense of guilt with that of his father, and his feeling that somehow his own rebellion was to be identified with that of his father prepared the way for the initial recovery of freedom, which issued from his own inner struggle, in the religious experience of 1838. In retrospect, traces of this movement can be seen in the Journal entries after 1835. In 1836 he wrote, we can hardly tell with how much personal concern, that conversion was a slow process; one had need of patience.[14] A little later he concluded that since Christianity had been so watered down that its central themes and concepts had almost lost their meaning, what was needed "was to win back the lost power and meaning of words."[15] By December of 1837 Kierkegaard had moved even closer to a positive identification with Christianity. He wrote: "I think that if ever I become seriously a Christian I shall be most ashamed of not having done so before, of having wished to try everything else first."[16] And within a few months he added: "If Christ is to come and take up his abode in me, it must happen according to the title of today's

Gospel in the Almanac: Christ came in through locked doors."[17] That these thoughts were an accurate presentiment of things to come is made clear by the decisive religious experience of May 19, 1838, an experience which represented the beginning of a kind of prodigal's return both to his earthly father and to Christianity. He was soon able to write: "I mean to labor to achieve a far more inward relation to Christianity; hitherto I have fought for its truth while in a sense standing outside it."[18] This declaration of intent in 1838 might well represent the whole direction of Kierkegaard's struggle in the remaining seventeen years of his life.

Another decisive step in this struggle was taken after the break in his engagement to Regine. In 1841 he said: "When the bonds were broken my thoughts were these: either you throw yourself into the wildest kind of life—or else become absolutely religious, but it will be different from the parsons' mixture."[19] Thus Kierkegaard had moved from a negative relationship to Christianity, through a positive intellectual interest in and defense of the faith, toward a more inward and existential identification with Christianity. He had already made this movement by the time he undertook his serious work as an author. There is no doubt that, when he came to review his work in *The Point of View* some years later, he was not reading something back from this later period when he characterized himself as a religious author from the beginning. In his explanation he does of course give the impression at times that he had understood and planned self-consciously the particular direction that his authorship was to take. Nevertheless, he himself corrected this impression when he wrote: "I can now understand it [the development of his authorship] and yet cannot by any means say that at the instant of commencing it I understood it so precisely. . . ."[20] And "So it is that I understand everything now. From the beginning I could not thus survey what has been in fact my own development."[21] These passages are more in keeping with Kierkegaard's own dictum that life can only be understood backward though it must be lived forward.[22]

Thus at the beginning of his authorship Kierkegaard thought of his relationship to Christianity in a positive fashion and he looked upon himself as a religious author. As early as 1842 he wrote that his readers could hardly have any inkling of his real motive for *Either/Or* and would hardly be able to understand what he meant if he had revealed to them that he regarded this book as a "good work."[23] In the next year he spoke of his purpose in life as that of presenting "the truth . . . in such a way as simultaneously to destroy all possible authority."

By ceasing to have authority, by being in the greatest possible degree unreliable in the eyes of man, I present the truth and put them in a contradictory position from which they can only save themselves by making the truth their own. Personality is only ripe when a man has made the truth his own whether it is Balaam's ass speaking or a laughing jack-ass with his loud laugh, an apostle or an angel.[24]

This goal of serving the truth and this strategy of making his readers aware of the truth in such a way that they themselves had to take some decisive stand continued to be Kierkegaard's goal and strategy throughout the remainder of his life, but it came to be understood by him in changing terms as his own relationship to the Christian faith deepened. This continuity in Kierkegaard's understanding of his role as an author within the context of his own changing relation to the Christian faith can be clearly demonstrated by the following series of brief quotations ranging through the eleven years from 1843 to 1854:

I wish to make people aware so that they do not squander and dissipate their lives.[25]

I have chosen to serve the truth . . . to raise the price [of Christianity] and if possible to whisper to every individual what the demands could be.[26]

All my terrific work as an author is one great thought and it is: to wound from behind.[27]

My whole life is an epigram calculated to make people aware.[28]

My very humble work is: to make people aware. I admit that I dare not do anything more—yet I am a cry of alarm.[29]

My task is: to make room that God may come, not authoritatively but through suffering.[30]

Within Kierkegaard's understanding of his own relationship to Christianity there are internal contradictions which are reflected in his view of his own work as an author. At times he thought his relationship to Christianity required that he be a *maieuticer*—a Socratic teacher.[31] The age needed education, and "God chose a man who also needed to be educated, and educated him *privatissime* so that he might be able to teach others from his own experience."[32] At other times Kierkegaard looked upon himself as the poet of the Christian faith, but the mark of a poet is that he does not live in the categories which he depicts.[33] Did Kierkegaard think of himself as more than a poet? Part of the difficulty in answering this question is that Kierkegaard was extremely sensitive about claiming too much for himself. He regarded it as a pretension to claim that he had achieved the heights of the Christian life depicted in his own works. Nevertheless, it is possible to trace the movement in his inner struggle as he is drawn closer and closer to becoming like that which he loved. Kierkegaard's inner wrestling with himself and with his melancholy represent a growing self-knowledge and a growing openness to God. Thus in 1847 after the publication of *Works of Love* he wrote:

I now feel the need of approaching nearer to myself in a deeper sense, by approaching nearer to God in the understanding of myself . . . I must come to grips with my melancholy. [I must try really to] think out the idea of my melancholy together with God here and now. That is how I must get rid of my melancholy and bring Christianity closer to me.[34]

A poet? Yes, but more than a poet. In reflecting on his own education in Christianity, Kierkegaard wrote: "I succeeded in carrying myself along so that I do not merely busy myself intellectually and poetically in representing what Christianity is."[35] From his second great religious experience in 1848 until the end, he gradually grew in his capacity for openness. He understands that in his writing he must give a personal and direct witness to what Christianity is; that he must identify himself openly with its cause. Echoing the passage quoted from the period eight years earlier, Kierkegaard wrote in 1849: "I have learnt to bear witness to Christianity, but not in the same way as all the parsons' trash does."[36] And yet, there were doubts in his mind. Perhaps, after all, he wondered, his personal existence was a purely poetic existence—"perhaps I might not after all become a Christian."[37] This doubt which is in Kierkegaard's mind is to be understood · against the exalted character of Christianity which he himself had depicted under the guise of Anti-Climacus, the pseudonym which represented the Christian faith to an extraordinary degree. In his own person Kierkegaard thought of himself as "quite a simple Christian." "I have never maintained," he wrote, "and do not maintain, that I am a Christian in any exceptional degree. It has been my task to depict Christianity. I have never maintained my action was an attempt to be a perfect Christian; this is why I have taken up a poetic attitude in my presentation of Christianity."[38] Real Christianity is self-denial, sobriety. It is "too exalted for me—I have enjoyed many many pleasures. I can only praise and extol strict Christianity."[39] Kierkegaard was one who in fear and trembling hardly dared call himself a Christian because of what this would seem to imply about his life.[40]

Though Kierkegaard did not alter his claim to being "only a simple Christian," his life took a turn in its last years which transformed his own mode of existence far beyond anything which he could call a poet's existence. In an entry dated May 18, 1851, Kierkegaard wrote: "I prayed to God that something new might be born within me. . . . Something new was born in me: for I now understand my duty as an author in quite a different sense to the direct spreading of religiousness."[41] His new understanding of his role in relation to Christianity now brought him to the front as a prophet of Christianity within Christendom. He moved on to the attack against the mediocrity of bourgeois Christianity in the name of a sterner and, as he believed, a more accurate understanding of New Testament faith.

The development of Kierkegaard's sense of personal vocation in which he comes to see the meaning of his own life and work is the reflection of the still deeper and more inward movement which he himself terms his "God-relationship." This movement, this God-relationship, can only be described as the process of "becoming a Christian," using the categories which Kierkegaard himself employed, for in his work as an author he was indeed charting and reflecting upon the course of his own life. "Becoming a Christian" defines the central movement of Kierkegaard's own life; it was this movement which served to define and determine both the content of his work as an author and his own sense of personal vocation. The movement itself, the God-relationship, the becoming a Christian, took place within a context shaped by certain focal relationships which were of decisive import, namely, the relationships to his father, to Regine Olsen, and to the *Corsair* controversy. These relationships became, as it were, leitmotivs woven in and through the central theme of his life.

KIERKEGAARD'S RELATION TO HIS FATHER

It would be difficult to exaggerate the influence of Michael Pedersen Kierkegaard on his youngest son. The father had been a prosperous merchant; he had retired in his fortieth year to spend his time in study, meditation, and theological discussion. Already in his fifties when Soren was born, possessed of a deeply religious pietistic nature, he was a man of great intellectual power. He had a rich imagination and enormous dialectical skill, and yet, as his son said, he was the most melancholy man he had ever known.[42]

Commenting on his father's death in his Journal, Kierkegaard wrote of his own early years:

To such a degree is the whole foreground of my life enveloped in the darkest melancholy and in the clouds of a deeply brooding misery—no wonder that I am what I am. . . . A fundamental melancholy, a tremendous dowry of suffering, and this, in the deepest sense sad, as a child educated by a melancholy old man. . . ."[43]

The father's education of the son was unorthodox and yet powerful in shaping the view of life and Christianity which the son was later to demonstrate. It was powerful too in developing the imagination and dialectical skill with which the son was himself so richly gifted. In the Journals, and in autobiographical sections of his books, there are indications of the kind of childhood training Kierkegaard had. He tells of his imaginary walks with his father, a "very severe man," who in walking with him up and down the room would describe all that they saw, so accurately, vividly, and explicitly that he would become as fatigued as if he had been a whole day out of doors. The son learned this magic power from his father so that the walk became a dialogue. Kierkegaard tells of how he was permitted to listen to his father's philosophical and theological discussions with friends. The son came to have the same fascination in dialectic that other children get from poetry or fairy tales.

Still stranger for a child was the father's method of inculcating religion, a method which may be symbolized by citing Kierkegaard's account in Training in Christianity.[44] The father places a picture of the Crucifixion among some other pictures of childhood heroes—Napoleon, William Tell, a huntsman. He shows the child one picture after another until they come to the picture of the crucified One. As if reminiscing Kierkegaard wrote:

The child will not at once nor quite directly understand this picture, and will ask what it means, why he hangs like that on a tree. So you explain to the child that this is a cross, and that to hang on it means to be crucified, and that in that land crucifixion was not only the most painful death penalty but was also an ignominious mode of execution employed only for the grossest malefactors. What impression will that make upon the child? The child will be in a strange state of mind, it will surely wonder that it could occur to you to put such an ugly picture among all the other lovely ones, the picture of a gross malefactor among all these heroes and glorious figures.

And then the child will ask: "Who is he? What did he do?" Then tell the child that this crucified man is the Saviour of the world. Yet to this he will not be able to attach any clear conceptions; so tell him merely that this crucified man was the most loving person that ever lived.

And what will the impression of this story be upon the child?

First and foremost surely this, that he has entirely forgotten the other pictures you have showed him; for now he had got something entirely different to think about. And now the child will be in the deepest amazement at the fact that God did nothing to prevent this being done; or that this was done without God raining down fire from heaven (if not earlier, at least at the last minute) to prevent His death. . . . That surely was the first impression. But by degrees, the more the child reflected upon the story, the more his passion would be aroused, he would be able to think of nothing but weapons and war—for the child would have decided that when he grew up he would slay all these ungodly men who had dealt thus with the loving One; that was his resolve, forgetting that it was 1,800 years ago they lived.

Then when the child became a youth he would not have for-

gotten the impression of childhood, but he would now understand it differently, he would know that it was not possible to
carry out what the child—overlooking the 1,800 years—had
resolved to do; but nevertheless he would think with the same
passion of combating the world in which they spat upon the
Holy One, the world in which they crucify love and beg acquittal
for the robber.

Then when he became older and mature he would not have
forgotten the impression of childhood, but he would understand
it differently. He would no longer wish to smite; for, said he,
"I should attain to no likeness with Him the humble One, who did
not smite even when He Himself was smitten." No, he wished
now only one thing, to suffer in some measure as He suffered in
this world. . . .

Kierkegaard's inner development of mind and spirit was
related to his father in another decisive way. Quite as powerful as the pervasive influence of his father's methods of
education, of his severity, his melancholy, and his own way
of understanding Christianity were particular events in the
life of Michael Pedersen Kierkegaard. These events tied
father and son together in a peculiar way. and influenced the
son's thought and self-understanding to a degree difficult to
measure. In the deepest recesses of his own life the father
harbored a secret. When this secret was discovered by the
son, it first produced a rebellion, and later its revelation drew
the two men closer together. Whether we accept at face
value the speculations that the secret which brought about
the "great earthquake" in Kierkegaard's life was the fact
that his father had, as a young shepherd boy, stood on the
top of a Jutland hill and cursed God or whether we choose
to believe that, after the death of his first wife, the father had

in passionate rebellion against God raped the servant woman who became his second wife and the mother of his children does not make an essential difference. The discovery of some such fact by the son and the later confession of the secret by the father came to make the son share with his father the feeling that the whole family lived under a curse. It served to foster the son's own melancholy. His own pre-disposition, the events and experiences of his life thus far, and this revelation taken together led him to feel that he was himself an exception. He came to believe that he was unable to lead a normal life or to escape his own shut-up-ness by revealing himself fully in communion with another human being. It drove him first away from his father and from the faith he represented, and it paved the way for the reconciliation and deeper identification with his father which was the prelude and no doubt one of the initiating factors which led to the decisive religious experience shortly after his twenty-fifth birthday. He wrote of his inner transformation in these words:

There is an indescribable joy which enkindles us as inexplicably as the apostle's outburst comes gratuitously: "Rejoice I say unto you, and again I say rejoice."—Not a joy over this or that but the soul's mighty song "with tongue and mouth, from the bottom of the heart": "I rejoice through my joy, in, at, with, over, by, and with my joy"—a heavenly refrain, as it were, suddenly breaks off our other song; a joy which cools and refreshes us like a breath of wind, a wave of air, from the trade wind which blows from the plains of Mamre to the everlasting habitations.[45]

KIERKEGAARD'S RELATION TO REGINE OLSEN

In the midst of Kierkegaard's movement away from his father and from Christianity, in the midst of the intensification of his feeling that he and his family were somehow exceptions, Kierkegaard fell deeply in love. He had first met Regine Olsen at the home of some friends in 1837, but she was only fourteen years old. Kierkegaard waited, began to court her, and became engaged to her three years later. Not only was he deeply in love with her, but his engagement symbolized for him the possibility of a normal human life. Yet almost as soon as the engagement was made he saw that he had made a mistake. Much has been written in an attempt to get at Kierkegaard's reasons for breaking the engagement —in trying to discover the precise nature of his "thorn in the flesh." Whether it was his deep melancholy, sexual impotence, his inability to reveal himself and the sins of his past life fully, his acute awareness of the incommensurability of personalities so different as his and Regine's, or his continued sense of being an exception may never be known. Suffice it to say that this event became one of the focal experiences through which Kierkegaard came to understand himself and the meaning of personal existence. For a year he tried to determine how best to break off the relationship. Finally, he decided to so misrepresent himself to Regine that she might no longer want to marry him. Then the blame for the rupture might rest on him. This action was decisive for his life and work. He soon sailed for Berlin, and "from that moment," he wrote, "I dedicated my life with every ounce of my poor ability to the service of an idea."[46]

In the course of the next year Kierkegaard embarked on a prolific authorship in "the service of an idea." One work followed another in which he was both exploring the meaning of his own life and attempting to move others to the same kind of self-discovery and deepening of personal existence.

In part this movement of thought was a reaction against romanticism and Hegelianism; in part it was a probing into the meaning and implications of the focal relationships of his own life; and in part it was a positive appropriation and interweaving of the historic categories of the Christian life with his own experience and thought. For a variety of reasons Kierkegaard had expected to complete his authorship with the large volume which he called *Concluding Unscientific Postscript*, published in 1846, and then, if he still lived, to devote himself to a country parish. Just as he was about to come to a decision, an event occurred which changed his plans radically and brought into being a new phase both in his authorship and in his life.

THE "CORSAIR" AFFAIR

The *Corsair* was a scandal-mongering weekly paper full of gossip and ridicule of the important people of the day. In his Journal Kierkegaard characterized both its methods and its popularity:

The ancients amused themselves by making men fight wild beasts, the baseness of modern times is more subtle. But there have been sacrifices and women have shed tears in silence (the wives and daughters of the persecuted), and in the meanwhile the grins broadened and the circulation rose. The victims went aside and died, and none remarked it; the women hid their tears, and none remarked it; for those who suffered naturally did everything in their power to conceal it.[47]

For some time Kierkegaard had been considering leveling an attack at the editors and their policies; not only did he condemn the demoralizing character of the sheet, but he resented the praise his own work had received in some of its issues. Then, one of the *Corsair*'s anonymous editors, P. L. Möller, for reasons of his own, published a critical review of some of Kierkegaard's writing, which Kierkegaard felt to be more of an attack on him personally than on his work. Kierkegaard replied to this attack effectively, but in so doing he identified Möller as one of the mainstays of the *Corsair* staff, comparing Möller's attack to typical *Corsair* slander. "Would that I might get into the *Corsair!* It is really bad for a poor author to stand so singled out in Danish literature, that . . . he is the only one not abused there."[48] The *Corsair* was quick to reply, and a running exchange began between Kierkegaard and its editors. The *Corsair*'s attack took the form of personal ridicule, and Kierkegaard soon found himself held up as a public joke. No one joined him in his attack; no one came to his defense.

Kierkegaard's experience in the *Corsair* controversy was as significant for his life and thought as was his engagement to Regine Olsen. He felt even more strongly than before that he was an exception—that ordinary human pursuits were closed to him. The country parish had now become an impossibility. It would be regarded by the public as a retreat, an escape. He came also to a clear understanding of his own capacity to venture out, to take a stand in action as well as in the realm of ideas; he was confirmed in his conviction that he who speaks the truth will have to suffer for the truth. What he later came to formulate so incisively under the Christian category of suffering, what had been first introduced to him in his early religious training in terms of the picture of a suffering and humiliated Christ, he now experienced personally with a sharpness unknown to him before.

In the years following the *Corsair* incident Kierkegaard moved toward greater self-definition in his own relation to the Christian faith—to a clearer understanding of the existential categories of the faith, to a sense of openness where he himself could speak out as a witness for the truth. Finally, he was led to his prophetic denunciation of the mediocrity of bourgeois Christianity. One of the occasions for this new movement had to do with a public controversy over Adolf Peter Adler, a parish minister who claimed to have received a direct revelation of Christ. Adler had been regarded as deranged and had been deposed from his ecclesiastical office. Kierkegaard used Adler's claims and his published works as a means of analyzing the confusion within the Christendom of his day and for clarifying his own relation to the faith and his role in relation to Christendom.

The second impetus toward the new movement in life and thought came through his religious experience of Easter week 1848. Behind this experience as behind the other great conversion experience of Kierkegaard's life in 1838 there lay a long, intense, and complicated inner struggle. To one who would understand Kierkegaard's passionate recourse to prayer these events may be taken as representative of the depths of his experience. The *Corsair* affair, the Adler controversy in which he had probed the problem of religious authority, his own continued sense of sin and guilt, the profound and pervasive melancholy whose power he seemed unable to shake, confronted him again with the problem of his own God-relationship. This time the confrontation centered around the question of the existential appropriation of the forgiveness of sins. Even in 1847 there had been a kind of premonition that some great change was about to occur in his life. By Easter of the next year the metamorphosis had begun. In his Journal he wrote: "My whole being is changed. My reserve and self-isolation is broken—I must speak."[49] And then: "Now, with God's help, I shall be myself. I believe that Christ will help me to be victorious over my melancholy. . . ."[50] But a few days later he wrote: "No, no, my self-isolation cannot be broken, at least not now."[51] Little by little, however, Kierkegaard came to know God's forgiveness in a deeply personal way. His belief in the forgiveness of sins came to mean "that here in time the sin is forgotten by God, that it is true that God really forgets."[52]

And now, now that in many ways I have been brought to the last extremity, now (since last Easter, though with intervals) a hope was awakened in my soul that God may desire to resolve the fundamental misery of my being. That is to say, now I am in faith in the profoundest sense. Faith is the immediacy after reflection. As a poet and thinker I have represented all things in the medium of the imagination, myself living in resignation. Now life comes closer to me, or I am closer to myself.—To God all things are possible, that thought is now, in the deepest sense, my watch-word, has acquired a significance in my eyes which I had never imagined it could have.[53]

As a consequence of these experiences Kierkegaard moved into a more open and direct advocacy of the Christian faith. He became a witness for the truth. Little by little his new role led him to a direct and sharper attack on the Christendom of his day. It became clear to him that the leadership of the church was either unaware or unwilling to admit how far official Christianity was from New Testament faith. Kierkegaard was held back from a direct attack on the church so long as Mynster, his father's old pastor and revered family friend, still lived and remained the responsible head of the state church. When Mynster died, however, Kierkegaard brought his dialectic to bear in powerful denunciation. He himself died in November, 1855, after a fall while in the midst of his battle as a defender of Christianity against the established church.

Chapter 2

BASIC THEMES

The persistent theme of all Kierkegaard's productive work is the meaning of personal existence—the problem of becoming a Christian. For him personal existence is essentially self-realization, but self-realization in its deepest and most profound sense. Personal existence is process; it is becoming; it is act. It may be debated whether a human being really "exists" in Kierkegaard's sense of the term unless he is in the process of becoming a Christian (in Kierkegaard's sense of becoming a Christian), but certainly for him the meaning of personal existence becomes clear only to one who is in the process of becoming a Christian, and, therefore, a description of this process is the nearest one can come to grasping the meaning of personal existence apart from the direct experience of becoming a Christian. The meaning of personal existence only becomes clear in the clarification of what it means to become a Christian, and practically all of Kierkegaard's work may be looked upon as contributing to such clarification.

Briefly and simply Kierkegaard's answer to the question of what it means to be a Christian might be stated as follows: To become a Christian is to become aware of one's innermost individuality or self. To become a Christian is to become a *single one*, an individual. No one can teach another how to become an individual. It is not something that can be communicated; it is only something that can be lived through for one's self. In dealing with the problem, therefore, Kierkegaard resorts to two methods. In his earlier writings he uses what he calls "indirect communication." Indirect communication means stating the alternatives concretely in such a way that the individual reader is moved through self-activity and decision toward the realization of his own individuality. It is the attempt to bring the reader to the point of choosing himself—the Kierkegaardian equivalent of the Socratic theme of knowing one's self. On certain occasions and particularly in his later phase Kierkegaard abandons indirect communication for direct testimony. The direct witness is not communication, but it may move one to the same kind of self-activity and decision toward which the method of indirect communication was aimed. In either case becoming a Christian is not a matter of knowledge; no one can teach it or do it for another. Since it involves self-realization of the individual at the deepest levels of self-existence, it must be lived through by the individual himself. This is one aspect of Kierkegaard's existentialism.

Kierkegaard develops his point of view in a very complex and subtle analysis of human life. Again he does not deal in abstract terms, but he represents the alternatives in concrete dramatic personal expressions. He does not say that a man may live in either this way or that, but rather with great artistic skill he describes a person who lives in this way or that. The alternatives presented are concrete; the decisions which are motivated are similarly concrete.

The alternatives depicted by Kierkegaard are sometimes called stages on life's way, sometimes spheres of existence.

In any case these stages or spheres do not represent a meta-physical analysis of the character of human existence, for no man exists in the abstract; no man exists metaphysically. Kierkegaard shows through concrete example how individual men live and think. The levels of life or stages or spheres are three: the aesthetic, the ethical, and the religious. There are two boundary zones corresponding to these three: irony, which is the boundary between the aesthetic and the ethical, and humor, which is the boundary between the ethical and the religious. In a way, these spheres of existence and the boundaries between them are ideal types, though they are meant to depict concrete ways in which individuals may live. No individual is a perfect example of any one type. In every individual the way of life may be mixed and confused, yet the dominant orientation of the life of the individual might be said to be either aesthetic or ethico-religious. Nor is the Kierkegaardian scheme of analysis meant to suggest an absolutely successive order, as if a person first lived on the aesthetic level of life, then in irony, then in the sphere of ethics, and so on. Yet personal existence must be described as movement toward the religious sphere of existence: it is movement away from the domination of the aesthetic in such a manner that the aesthetic is not rejected but is incorporated in a higher way of life in which the individual realizes himself more fully. Personal existence is constituted in the acts by which the individual moves away from the aesthetic toward the religious.

One way of understanding this movement toward the Christian life, toward authentic personal existence, is to understand what it is that Kierkegaard was reacting against.

In charting the course for personal existence, Kierkegaard is rejecting the reductionism of both romanticism and rationalism. For him, the chief enemies of personal existence are romantic aestheticism and rationalistic speculation. The true movement of life is away from the aesthetic and away from speculation, for both aestheticism and speculation stand in the way of self-realization and both result in the disappearance of authentic individuality.

THE AESTHETIC LEVEL

A person who lives on the aesthetic level is not an integral self; such a person lives in immediacy, determined by externals.[1] There is no inner integrity, no self-determination from within, no real continuity at the base of one's existence.[2] Such persons live for enjoyment.[3] They are on the surface of life: observers, spectators, tasters, but not serious participants. "The aesthetical in man is that by which he is immediately what he is. . . ."[4] Kierkegaard means by this statement that the aesthete, the one who lives for enjoyment, lives in the moment; everything is in the moment, which is to say that the moment is essentially nothing. Time is not really taken seriously.[5] To say that a person is determined from without is to say that the aesthete has no real freedom. The aesthete recognizes that there is choice, but choosing is not important to him.[6] Choices may be made, but they are not internalized, not taken seriously; they are not posited by the individual himself.[7] The individual person disappears, dissolves, in the mood created by the environment.[8] His center is on the periphery. He lives outside himself.[9] In the aesthete that which might constitute the self is only the "manifold concretion of its components."[10] There may be development, but development for the aesthete is becoming what one immediately is.[11] Enjoyment is the aim of life whether health, or beauty, or wealth, or glory, or station, or something else is seen as the highest good. Even where the requisite condition for such enjoyment lies within the individual, it is not posited by the individual as individual. Either the conditions lie outside or they lie in a segment of the person and, in that case, the personality is determined as a talent, e.g., the businessman, the mathematician, the poet, etc.[12]

Such a life, lived for enjoyment, Kierkegaard embodies in a number of sophisticated fictional characters: Victor Eremita, Constantine Constantius, the young man in *Either/Or*, the Ladies' Tailor, and Johannes the Seducer. These people do not live seriously; they have no real inner life, no real self. Life for them has no special significance. There is no real continuity in their lives; everything is in the moment.[13] The only continuity in their lives is that they are continually being bored, finding that they must always seek the freshness and immediacy of new pleasures. Such boredom can only end in apathy, indifference, and weariness with life, so that beneath the outward appearance there will be despair and bitterness.[14] Within the aesthetic stage there are many subsidiary levels. The differences may be extraordinary—"all the way from complete stupidity to the highest degree of cleverness."[15] Essentially it is the poet-existence, an escape from the demands of life and from serious concerned living.

In his various aesthetic writings Kierkegaard is attempting to show the shallowness of life at the aesthetic level in such a way (by indirect communication) that the reader himself will be moved to decide against it and in and through this decision to become aware of himself and realize himself at a deeper level. It may not become immediately apparent what this deeper level is, or how a man is to reach it, but the movement away from the aesthetic is a movement toward the realization of personal existence. It is movement in the direction of Christian faith.

RATIONALISM AND SPECULATION

The other great enemy of authentic personal existence was rationalism or speculation, represented in its most advanced form by Hegel and his followers. The speculative thinker belongs within the aesthetic sphere of existence, but the importance of speculation as an enemy of true existence justifies special analysis of Kierkegaard's views at this point. Where his aesthetic works were primarily an attack on aestheticism, his *Philosophical Fragments* and *Concluding Unscientific Postscript* are in large part attacks on Hegelianism.[16] Like the aesthete in the narrower sense, the speculative philosopher not only fails to realize himself in authentic personal existence but his world view is an inadequate representation of reality.

Against Hegel and his followers Kierkegaard levels two acute criticisms. In the first place, he charges them with giving a false account of what it means to exist; in the second, he accuses them of so watering down the truth of Christianity that men no longer know what it means to become a Christian. On the one hand, Hegel leaves out of his account of reality the most important characteristics of existence, and, on the other, he reduces Christianity to a doctrine, leaving out the distinctive experiential categories by which a person becomes a Christian.

Perhaps the most serious specific charge that Kierkegaard makes against Hegel is that of confusing thought with existence. In the *Postscript* he writes: "The philosophical principle of identity is precisely the opposite of what it seems to be; it is the expression for the fact that thought has deserted existence altogether. . . ."[17] Hegel has forgotten what it means to live; he has identified existence with a conceptual formulation of existence; he has reduced existence to abstract thought. According to Kierkegaard, this fundamental confusion of thought with existence results in important subsequent errors.

One of the errors which results from such an identification of thought and existence lies in the method to which it leads. If there is an identity between thought and existence, then thought or reason is a dependable way of discovering the nature of existence. Kierkegaard repudiates this principle in repudiating the ground for it, and for this he has been accused of irrationalism. Reason is adequate for certain tasks, especially for the task of discovering its own inadequacies and its limits, but it is not adequate for the task of representing existence. Existence literally cannot be thought. To think existence is to abrogate it.

Existence . . . is a difficult category to deal with; for if I think it I abrogate it, and then I do not think it. It might therefore seem to be the proper thing to say that there is something which cannot be thought, namely, existence, but the difficulty persists, in that existence itself combines thinking with existing, in so far as the thinker exists.[18]

To think existence as Hegel tries to do is to seek objective truth about existence, but objective truth whether historical or philosophical is disinterested truth. In trying to get at objective truth the thinker tries to leave himself out as much as possible. Reason not only abstracts from concrete events, but it tries to abstract from the thinker himself. Man is turned into an observer. Such truth as man finds is not "truth for him"; it is universal; it is general; and it is only approximate.[19] The objective disinterested approach may be appropriate under certain conditions and for dealing with certain kinds of problems, but for Kierkegaard it is not appropriate for dealing with the problem of existence or that of how to become a Christian.[20] The really existential problems in which decision, infinite interest, appropriation are necessary cannot be dealt with in this way. Kierkegaard shows clearly the ineffectiveness of the speculative approach to such existential questions as: What does it mean to be immortal? What does it mean that I am to thank God for the good he bestows on me? What does it mean to get married? What does it mean to die? Abstract thought distorts the existential quality of the question by leaving out the subjective thinker whose deep personal concern the question is.

The identity of thought and existence leads to a philosophy of immanence in which distinctions, contradictions, discontinuities are blurred, annulled, or are missed entirely. For speculative philosophy everything is of a piece.[21] All thinking is rooted in the principle of immanence.[22] There is no real discontinuity and so no real transcendence in Hegel's philosophy. Hegel's dialectic is not a dialectic of existence but of thought; the contradictions are resolved. More than this, Hegelian philosophy rejects the principle of contradiction. Such a rejection would be defensible if Hegel proposed only a system of logic, but he is wrong when he attempts to abrogate the final either/or in existence.[23]

Not only does a philosophy of identity reduce the concrete to the abstract and objective, but such a philosophy also reduces contingency to necessity. There is neither real novelty nor real freedom when the attempt is made to think existence.[24] The speculative thinker thinks in terms of finality and the System.[25] Everything is logicized. Within the System there is no real becoming and hence no freedom or novelty. The various parts of the System are related to each other in terms of necessity. Yet this expression of the nature of reality in the abstract system when compared to reality itself is only possibility; it is because speculative thought changes everything into possibility that it belongs within the aesthetic sphere. As Kierkegaard writes in the *Postscript:*

Abstract thought considers both possibility and reality, but its concept of reality is a false reflection since the medium within which the concept is thought is not reality, but possibility. Abstract thought can get hold of reality only by nullifying it, and this nullification of reality consists in transforming it into possibility. . . . All knowledge about reality is possibility.[26]

Perhaps the most serious results of the philosophical identification of thought and existence have been mentioned. The one is the elimination of the existing individual; the other is the reduction of real becoming to a merely conceptual becoming, which from Kierkegaard's point of view is not becoming at all.

In the tremendous effort to reach objective truth, the subject eliminates himself as an existing individual. He forgets that he exists. Objective thinking is wholly indifferent to subjectivity, says Kierkegaard.[27] But the thinker who leaves himself out of his thought can hardly explain life. A thinker can leave himself out of his thinking through a sheer striving for objectivity, or perhaps through identifying the subject and object through mediation as Fichte did, or even through dissolving the individual in the race or in the species. In this last case the individual is less important than the race; he becomes just a representative or an example. Such a view of the individual runs contrary to the notion that the individual is created in the image of God, a notion which implies that the individual is above the race.[28]

If speculative philosophy loses the individual "exister," how can it expect to know what reality is, much less what it means to realize personal existence. All reality known by reason is turned into possibility, and the only reality to which man has more than a cognitive relationship is his own reality, his own existence. If speculative thought leaves out of its consideration the only reality which cannot be turned into possibility through thought (though thought of course cannot know it either), it can hardly expect to penetrate very deeply into reality. Hegel's philosophy cannot help anyone to understand himself, says Kierkegaard, and yet that is surely an absolute condition for all other kinds of understanding.[29]

If the speculative thinker eliminates the real individual from the system which thought thinks, he also eliminates the becoming, the movement by which the individual realizes and maintains his individuality. Hegel claims that his is a philosophy of becoming, of movement.[30] According to Kierkegaard, all that Hegel says about process and becoming is illusory.[31] Kierkegaard's point is that you cannot think becoming or movement. The categories of logic are static. The introduction of movement into logic is sheer confusion.[32] Reality is the transition from possibility to actuality. Thought is the transition from reality to possibility. The one is real movement and becoming; the other is merely conceptual. The one cannot be stated in the language of abstraction; the other is constituted by language and language alone.[33] This misunderstanding of the nature of real becoming leads Hegel to a misunderstanding of history and time. History is not understood as real becoming; it is understood from the point of view of a finality that excludes all becoming.[34] Time is not taken seriously. As a philosopher of immanence Hegel abolishes the real distinction between time and eternity. The moment is not important, since the eternal is all around.

Because abstract thought is *sub specie aeterni* it ignores the concrete and the temporal, the existential process, the predicament of the existing individual arising from his being a synthesis of the temporal and the eternal situated in existence.[35]

Thus the sharp distinction between time and eternity is annulled. There is no real becoming; time is not accentuated, for time is understood not as movement, not as involving futurity, but as pastness. The speculative philosopher desires in time to be merely eternal. Kierkegaard writes that speculative philosophy resolves the distinction between "here" and "hereafter" into pure being. This is one of the most important distinctions which must be preserved if reality is not to be falsified, for all the other distinctions converge around this one.[36] Speculative philosophy never really comes to terms with existence as existing; it sees the fact of existing only in its pastness; "existence is a transitory factor resolved into pure being."[37] This falsification of reality is the result of the identification of thought and existence, an identification which leads Hegel and his followers to regard actuality as necessity, thus denying the contingency and freedom which produce real becoming, not mere logical transition. In the interest of freedom Kierkegaard protests against Hegel's identity of the necessary and the actual. "When the past becomes actual does it become more necessary that it was?" he asks.[38]

Just as the Hegelian philosophy failed to represent reality, it failed to represent Christianity and for many of the same reasons. Speculative philosophy makes Christianity into a doctrine, something to be understood or known, something which is a matter of objective truth. In so doing, it has emasculated the Christian concepts, bringing bankruptcy to the world of the spirit. Modern discourse about Christianity, says Kierkegaard, has lost its vigor; it has been reduced to a toothless twaddle.[39] To understand Christianity in the sense of knowing it is to misunderstand it, for Christianity is not a matter of knowledge. Hegelianism made it easy to be a Christian when it made Christianity a matter of knowledge. For Kierkegaard, Christianity is precisely the opposite of knowledge; it is not objective truth; it is the intensification of subjectivity; it is infinitely difficult; it is appropriation—decision. "Christianity is not a doctrine, but an existential contradiction."[40] Speculative thought, however, deprives reality of its inherent contradictions. The contradictions are essential for Christianity; they provide the tension, the heightening of passion, and the dialectic which are the means by which and through which an individual becomes a Christian. Christianity is the opposite of speculation; it has nothing to do with mediation; it maintains the discontinuities which are essential to existence. The speculative philosophy, on the other hand, so interprets Christianity as to reduce the essential categories of the Christian faith: sin, suffering, guilt, the Absurd, the Absolute Paradox, faith, the offense, etc., to matters of knowledge. The speculative thinker does not exist in these categories; he thinks them, and this is precisely the opposite of what it means to be or to become a Christian. Suffering, inwardness, passion, decision, will, belief, the trial and struggle, infinite interest—all are lost for the speculative thinker who remains within immanence. The speculative thinker thinks it is possible to have a direct relationship with God; faith is seen as simple immediacy. For Kierkegaard, on the other hand, only an indirect relationship with God is possible, for God is incognito. "The philosopher contemplates Christianity for the sake of interpenetrating it with speculative thought. . . . But . . . suppose that Christianity is subjectivity, an inner transformation, an actualization of inwardness,"[41] then the infinite incommensurability of the two positions is comic. Objectively Christianity has no existence, for an objective knowledge of the "truth" of Christianity would be untruth. A real relation to Christianity is not cognitive but means appropriation and inner transformation.

BECOMING A CHRISTIAN—A SYNOPTIC VIEW

To become a Christian is to move toward authentic personal existence. It is to move away from the aesthetic sphere including the rationalistic objective speculative approach to the meaning of life. Existence within the aesthetic sphere is minimal personal existence if it can be called personal existence in any Kierkegaardian sense of the word at all. Within the aesthetic sphere the individual does not "realize" himself either in the sense of becoming aware of himself as an individual or in the sense of actualizing his individuality. As an individual moves beyond the aesthetic level understood either as aestheticism or speculation, he moves toward the ethico-religious level and in the process becomes an individual, a person, on ever deeper levels of existence. It is this movement, this process, this becoming, this actualization and intensification of subjectivity which leads toward the Christian life. It is this movement which is personal existence. Many Kierkegaardian commentators have stressed the stages themselves, but the stress should be put on the movement within the stages or between the stages. Personal existence is not static; it is *active* becoming, *active* self-realization.

The second sphere of existence is the ethical. It represents struggle and victory. Decision and choice and a positive relation to life are its characteristics. Those who live on this level attempt to realize the universal, for the ethical represents the universal demand: what every man ought to do. In the ethical stage a man acts; he is concerned; he is interested; he lives seriously. In acting, in being concerned, in choosing and deciding, he is actually constituting himself. One cannot choose anything concrete without the prior decision to choose, that is, to live above the aesthetic level. This act of decision, as well as consequent decisions, demands that one really become aware of himself *as a self* and that he choose himself in the very act of deciding to choose and in making concrete succeeding choices. It means the assumption of responsibility, and that implies the emergence of a responsible self.

The condition which makes possible the movement from the aesthetic to the ethical stage is what Kierkegaard calls "despair." Despair is not doubt; it is to the whole person what doubt is to the intellect; it affects the whole person. Despair is itself a choice; it is the beginning of the decision which marks the break with the aesthetic and the leap to the ethical sphere.

The third level is the religious, and here self-realization or individuality or subjectivity receives an even more concrete expression. The religious level is divided for Kierkegaard into what he calls Religion A and Religion B, the religion of immanence and Christianity. Religion A and Religion B are forms of religious orientation, not forms of institutional religion. An individual lives in the religious sphere when he realizes that the ethical-universal is not binding—that there are individuals who are exceptions to the universal demands—in religious terms, that there is a God-relationship which is private and peculiar to each individual. At this stage the choices which constitute the self are on a new level of inwardness. The relationship to God is personal and incommunicable. In Religion A, God is found within the inner life. Man's task is not to realize the universal but to express his peculiar individual concrete relationship to God and in all his acts and decisions to express an absolute relationship to the Absolute and a relative relationship to the relative. The most acute expression of all this is within the inner life of man. It means that the individual's whole inner life should be transformed in terms of the absolute God-relationship.

Such a transformation means according to Kierkegaard three things: infinite resignation, suffering, and guilt. Infinite resignation means dying to the world, the renunciation of all relativities, seeking the Kingdom first. Suffering means that this is something man cannot do for himself. The transformation is a transformation *of* the self, but not *by* the self. It produces inner anguish. Guilt grows out of the experience of one's inability to carry through the infinite resignation. One becomes aware that one cannot exercise the absolute relationship to the Absolute. Each of these steps represents a further intensification of subjectivity, a further realization of what it means to be an individual.

In Religion A, the religion of immanence, the God-relationship is constituted within the individual. Here perhaps we are in a position to understand Kierkegaard's famous and often misunderstood dictum: *subjectivity is truth:* In this expression Kierkegaard is not talking about truth in the usual sense at all. By "truth" he means the character of the relationship to God. A man who really prays to an idol is nearer the "truth" than a man who merely goes through the motions in relation to the Christian God. When he says that in Religion A, the religion of immanence, subjectivity is truth, he is saying that for those who exist at this level, the relationship to God in one's inwardness as the absolute relationship to the Absolute, brought about by infinite resignation, suffering, and the consciousness of guilt, represents a true or valid relationship to God.

Is any further intensification of subjectivity possible beyond the religion of immanence? Can man become any more of an individual than he is at this stage? Is any further self-realization possible? To these questions Kierkegaard replies in the affirmative. Christianity represents the highest intensification of subjectivity possible. In appropriating its truth, an individual finally becomes aware of what it means to be a self, and, in becoming aware of what it means to be a self, he becomes that self through the grace of God. Christianity, for Kierkegaard, denies that subjectivity is truth—in the sense that subjectivity is truth for a man within Religion A. For Christianity, human subjectivity is not truth in this sense; in this sense, it is untruth; yet subjectivity is still truth, but in a different way. Just as the ethical attitude to life fails when one sees that he cannot realize the universal, so Religion A fails when one comes to the realization that God is not to be found within the inner life of man; that there is no identity of man's spirit and God. This conviction arises as man becomes aware that he is a sinner; that there is an abyss between him and God; that, as Kierkegaard puts it, there is an infinite qualitative difference between man and God.[42] Man does not become aware of this from within (and this is the sense in which subjectivity is untruth); he becomes aware of it only through Revelation, through the Paradox, through the conviction that what is wholly unacceptable to reason and thought has actually taken place. This paradox which is an offense to reason is that God, the Eternal, has become incarnate in a particular individual man, Jesus, in time. For Kierkegaard, time and eternity are utterly irreconcilable by reason. That the Eternal should have become incarnate in time, and in an individual man, that God should have put on human flesh is an absurdity from the point of view of reason; it is an offense to the understanding.

When a man accepts this absurdity, and he cannot accept it with his understanding or his reason, he becomes conscious of the tremendous gulf between himself and God. God is God and man is man and he is a sinner. Man accepts this Incarnation as a historical event only on the basis of faith, only by an act of decision, a leap. No amount of knowledge of the character of Jesus or about the historical events of his life can make a believer out of an individual. In the final analysis one believes in the Incarnation by faith alone, a faith which is both an act of the will and a gift of God. Faith is the belief that the Absurd has really happened, and every man must make the same leap of faith whether he was Jesus' historical contemporary or whether he is a modern man. In this sense we are all contemporaries of Christ. We all have the same opportunity; we are all presented with the same absurdity, the same offense, and we must all decide.

So it is that in Christianity through the consciousness of sin and faith in the Absurd and the Paradox the individual comes to the ultimate intensification of his own individuality. He sees himself as he really is, as a sinner, alone before God. To become a Christian means to reach this sphere of existence and to *continue* in this ultimate consciousness of what it means to be an individual, a sinner, alone before God, saved by faith in the Absurd, the Paradox. There is no resting place. Personal existence both "on the way" and "in faith" is a continual struggle, a continual risk, a continual actualization of individuality. There is no release in time. Eternity is grasped by man only as expectation.

Chapter 3

TOWARD THE CHRISTIAN LIFE

The movement of personal existence toward the Christian life is a movement toward freedom, through increasing freedom, by means of free decision. In this movement an individual exists in certain media. The character or quality of his existence can be indicated in terms of the media through which he is passing. There is no necessary sequence in the media of existence, though they represent the degree to which an individual realizes personal existence.

DESPAIR: THE EMERGENCE OF SELF-CONSCIOUSNESS

If a man is not conscious of himself as a self, he first becomes so through despair, because despair is essentially a lack of harmony and balance within the self. By becoming conscious of this lack of harmony and balance, man becomes conscious of the relationship which constitutes the self. The importance of despair for personal existence is well illustrated in these words from Kierkegaard's Journals: "It is perfectly true that only terror to the point of despair develops a man to his utmost—though of course many succumb during the cure; but it is also useful for a man to be handled as roughly as all that."[1]

Every aesthetic view of life is despair, and whether one knows it or not, if one lives aesthetically, one is in despair. The moment, however, that one is conscious of his despair there is a demand for a higher form of existence. Should an individual then will his own despair, i.e., will to accept his despair for what it is, recognizing that he is in the aesthetic, he emerges by that act of decision, not beyond despair, but beyond the aesthetic despair which is not conscious of itself. In the very act of choosing to recognize this despair for what it is, he begins to constitute himself as a self.[2] In this act freedom posits itself; by an act of freedom (choice, decision) he affirms his freedom. In choosing, a man gets beyond immediacy; the self he chooses is not his immediate self, for if it were, he would not be conscious of it. It is his own self in its eternal validity.[3]

In *Either/Or* the Judge sees despair as the means by which one can transcend the aesthetic sphere and exist ethically. Kierkegaard himself would agree with the Judge, yet this is not the ultimate goal. Consciousness of one's despair and willingness to accept one's self as despairing are not enough. The movement can be carried further and leads a man to deeper levels of self. To become conscious of one's despair *as sin before God* would be the deeper understanding.[4] Such an existential understanding of the true nature of despair at once involves the categories of the religious life and finally those of the Christian life itself. Therefore when the Judge says that "in choosing absolutely I choose despair, and in despair I choose the absolute for I myself am the absolute. I posit the absolute and I myself am the absolute; but in complete identity with this I can say that I choose the absolute which chooses me, that I posit the absolute which posits me" and goes on to say that the absolute is the self in its eternal validity, it must be observed that this is not truly a movement within the ethical or, better perhaps, that the term "posit" cannot mean "become" in any strict sense in this context.[5] This statement becomes clearer in the light of *Sickness unto Death*.

In *Sickness unto Death* Kierkegaard discusses the nature of despair more fully, relating it to the religious sphere as well as to the aesthetic and the ethical. He analyzes the different types of despair in a systematic but rather artificial manner. The self is a relating of body and soul, of infinite and finite, of possibility and necessity. Its sickness (despair) may be rooted in one or more of these constitutive relationships. In *Works of Love* Kierkegaard declares that despair is not something that happens to a man, like fortune or misfortune; it is rather a "disproportion" in man's inmost being.[6] In *Purity of Heart* he defines despair as "doublemindedness." The disproportion, the doublemindedness, the imbalance may take a variety of forms. A man may live too much in his imagination. This is a lack of balance in the direction of the infinite. Or another may be lost in worldliness; he is so much one of the crowd that he has lost his integrity and is not a true self. This is an imbalance in the direction of finitude. In the same fashion a man may fail to see himself as he really is in the direction of either necessity or possibility. If he is fatalistic, if he thinks everything is necessitated, or that nothing matters and all is trivial—this is despair. It is a disproportion within the self, for the self has real possibilities.[7] If he thinks nothing is impossible for him, he is again "unbalanced," and this imbalance is the character of despair.

Despair may also be regarded from the point of view of man's consciousness. It was so treated in *Either/Or*. If a man is unconscious of his having a self, he is certainly not conscious of any inner disproportion, and this too is despair,

despair at the aesthetic level. One may also be conscious of one's despair, of the disproportion within the structuring of the self, and still be in despair. For Kierkegaard there are several kinds of despair which are disclosed from this perspective. There is the despair of weakness. One despairs at not willing to be one's self. There is the despair of defiance in which one wills despairingly to be one's self.

Such disproportions have their psychological counterparts. They are felt as torment, as gnawing pain. Or despair may be felt as a hot incitement, a cold fire, or a growing canker "whose movement is constantly inward, deeper and deeper, in impotent self-consumption." The very fact that this is a torment which cannot be ended, which is "unto death" but never death itself, demonstrates that there is something eternal in man; it is a sign of the dignity of man as well as an indication, at its more advanced stages, of the depth of his sin. This feeling component of despair is not, however, a necessary part of its existence. Whether a man feels his despair is not essential, he is in despair all the same.[8]

The varieties of despair already considered can all be characterized within the definition of the human self, but despair appears in new proportions when the self is seen *before God.* It then appears as sin. Kierkegaard writes in *Sickness unto Death:*

Despair is potentiated in proportion to consciousness of self; but the self is potentiated in the ratio of the measure proposed for the self, and infinitely potentiated when God is the measure. The more conception of God, the more self; the more self, the more conception of God. Only when the self as this definite individual is conscious of existing before God, only then is it the infinite self; and then this self sins before God.[9]

Yet it appears that despair is sin in the strict sense only when a man is conscious that he is before God, and when he knows what that means. Real sin presupposes revelation of what sin is, and then "before God in despair not to will to be one's self, or before God in despair to will to be one's self."[10] Revelation is necessary to make despair sin, because no man can know what sin is by himself, for he is a sinner.

The despair which is sin is disobedience; it is man's wilful failure to ground himself transparently in God. Grounding one's self transparently in God is an equivalent expression for "faith." Sin's opposite therefore is faith, not virtue, and faith is the final answer to despair. In faith the self wills to be itself; it grounds itself transparently in the Power which constituted it by this kind of relationship to itself.

Despair, in the sense of the inner disorganization of the complex of relationships which constitute the self, is to be seen as one of the media of personal existence, one of the categories in the movement toward the Christian life. It characterizes the process of deepening subjectivity which is personal existence. The more self—the more despair; the more self-consciousness—the more despair. It is a sign of both the depths and the heights of personal existence. It is related to man's existence as a self, to his freedom, to his sin, to his being before God, and to his being constituted by God. At this point one might well ask: Is despair ever overcome completely? For Kierkegaard this would seem to be impossible. Despair might be said to be overcome in *moments* of faith, but these are only moments. So long as man remains in time he is a sinner, and so long as he is a sinner he despairs, and his despair serves to increase both his sin, his consciousness of sin, and his need for forgiveness.

Man is spirit in his essential nature. To say this is to say that there is a dimension in the individual's life which transcends bodily or physical life and psychical life. This dimension is spirit; it is what gives man "splendor"; it is his most precious possession. This "splendor" can be summed up in a single sentence which Scripture itself pronounces with authority: God has created man in His own image.[11] God is spirit; He is invisible, and it is this invisibility which is the very definition of spirit; man's invisible glory, the image of God in him is spirit, and the other name for spirit is *self*. Spirit is the combining factor in the synthesis of body and soul.[12] Spirituality, says Kierkegaard, is the power of a man's understanding over his life, which might be interpreted to mean that spirituality is the capacity for holding ideality and actuality together, for living in one's categories, for reduplication, for realizing the truth in one's individual existence.[13] "There is only one attestation of spirit, and that is the attestation of the spirit within one's self."[14] This spirit, this capacity, this witness is the self.

Kierkegaard's understanding of the self has been alluded to in the discussion of despair. Despair was a disproportion within the self. The self is not a substance; it is a dynamic relationship. It is not a simple relationship between two terms, but it is a peculiar kind of relationship between two terms which has the additional positive capacity to relate to itself. It has a reflexive character.[15] If such a characterization of the nature of selfhood is difficult to understand, a more fruitful approach may be that taken by Swenson and by Smith in contrasting the actual and the ideal self.[16] There is good justification for their procedure in *Either/Or* where

Kierkegaard writes: "The self which the individual knows is at once the actual self and the ideal self which the individual has outside himself as the picture in likeness to which he has to form himself and which, on the other hand, he nevertheless has in him since it is the self."[17] According to E. E. Smith, the self is power striving toward a goal; it is not static, nor is it primarily the locus of consciousness. It is the active interrelationship of ideal and actual self. Thus the self in reflective self-consciousness creates an ideal self which serves as the goal and guide of its movement. This is the way in which we are to understand the dictum: the more consciousness, the more self.[18] The more one strives toward the ideal self, the more the tension increases within the actual self. Thus the self is at one time two selves (in the sense of being or containing an actual and an ideal self) and one self (in the sense that only the actual self really exists, for the ideal self is its creation). So when Kierkegaard writes in *Sickness unto Death* that the self is a conscious synthesis of infinitude and finitude which relates itself to itself, whose task is to become itself, he is really saying that there is a self which relates itself (the actual self) to itself (the ideal self), and the task is to actualize the ideal. For the same reason Swenson can say that reality for Kierkegaard is the ethical synthesis of the ideal and the actual within the individual.[19] The self is always in tension, for it is a complex of contraries. The self is the dialectical synthesis of an expansive and a limiting factor. Finitude is the limiting factor and the infinite is the expanding factor expressing itself in man's imagination. Kierkegaard says that the task is to become concrete. One becomes concrete by moving away from one's self infinitely by infinitizing one's self and then returning to one's self infinitely by finitizing one's self.[20] One infinitizes one's self through the imagination. Imagination constructs an ideal self. But one must not remain in the realm of imagination; one should return to reality. That is to say the ideal self should be actualized, should be related to the former actual self so that the new self which emerges is the synthesis of the ideal and the actual. In existence or in the existent all the factors which go to make up the individual must be co-present; one cannot really live as a person in the world of thought or in the world of imagination as do the speculative thinker and the aesthete. To put Kierkegaard's understanding of the self in this way is simply to explain further what he means by the sentence already quoted from his Journals: "Spirituality is the power of a man's understanding over his life."

Kierkegaard's view of the problem of selfhood in relation to personal existence can also be put in terms of the concept integration or reintegration. For Kierkegaard the unifying power of personality is the inmost and holiest thing of all. The main theme of one of his best-loved discourses, *Purity of Heart*, can be characterized as attaining unity within the self. He himself describes the process as that of attaining unchangeableness. Perhaps too this is only another way of stating the meaning of another two of his important concepts, those of repetition and reduplication.

The same problem of self is discussed in still another way from the point of view of the ethicist in *Either/Or*. The self is again seen as that which gives unity to the individual. By virtue of the self man is not legion; the self gives continuity to becoming; it is personality and freedom. The self is freedom because it is born out of self-appropriation or self-choice. Choice of the self brings the self into existence, yet the fact that it could be chosen implies that it was there all along.[21] What we have previously called the actual self, we might here call the latent self or the dissociated self. When a man chooses to choose, we might say that he activates his latent self, or that he integrates his dissociated self. The new self is in one sense the same self that existed, for it was there all the time, and yet it is a new self, different by virtue of the fact that it is now active, now integrated—it has been chosen. As Kierkegaard puts it: "The choice permeates everything and transforms it."[22]

From such an account of the self it might appear that the self is self-constituted. In a negative sense that statement contains an element of truth, for the self for Kierkegaard is certainly not the product of social conditioning. From the very limited perspective of the ethicist, the statement would be true in the positive sense too. The ethical sphere is characterized by self-reliance; such self-reliance is not unrelated to God, but man's relation to God is represented by the universal ethical demands and in the ethical sphere one assumes that man is capable of realizing them. Just at this point the issue is sharply drawn. Man is incapable of realizing the universal ethical both because he has his own unique relationship to God which transcends the ethical norm and because he is a sinner. It is not a sin that man cannot realize the universal, but he cannot realize the universal because he is a sinner. Man can despair, but the leap of decision which can really meet despair is not a simple possibility. Man cannot deliver himself from bondage; he cannot pull himself up by his bootstraps. In order to realize this fact, Kierkegaard would say that man must leave the ethical realm; he must be emancipated from the universal ethical requirement. Such an emancipation, such a suspension of the ethical is fearful, for: "The terrible emancipation from the requirement of realizing the ethical, the heterogeneity of the individual with the ethical, this suspension from the ethical is Sin, considered as the state in which the human being is."[23] This movement toward recognition of one's self as a sinner brings a new depth of self-awareness, a new intensification of inwardness and subjectivity, a further realization of personal existence. This movement can be described not only in terms of the concepts of spirit or self or person but also in terms of the category of the individual which is their essential equivalent. The category of the individual Kierkegaard called "his category." Usually in his discussion of the individual, the single one, Kierkegaard intends to distinguish the individual from the crowd, the mass, the race, the species, but the "individual" is also set over against abstract universality. Kierkegaard declares that the individual is the category of the spirit, of spiritual awakening. It is the decisive Christian category. Christianity stands or falls with the category of the individual. Self-realization is becoming an individual. Personal existence is existence as a single one, as an individual. As Kierkegaard himself declares, the theme of the individual comes to evidence in one way or another throughout his work. In the pseudonymous works the individual is primarily the pre-eminent individual in the aesthetic sense, the distinguished person. In the edifying works the individual is what every man can be. It is in this sense that the individual might be called the concrete universal as opposed to the abstract universal. The crowd reduces the individual to a nonentity just as the speculative thinker does, yet the crowd is composed of individuals, and so, says Kierkegaard, "it must therefore be in every man's power to become what he is, an individual."[24] Christianity or personal existence in its fullest form is not aristocratic in the sense that it is open only on the basis of invidious distinctions of human life such as talent or genius. "Christianity is certainly accessible to all but—be it carefully noted—only provided everyone becomes an individual, becomes 'the individual.' "[25] The main condition of religiousness is to be a single individual man. The category of the individual is that through which, religiously speaking, all must pass. To this theme Kierkegaard returns again and again. "Art thou related to thyself as an individual?" he asks. "Art thou conscious of thy relationship as an individual— to God?" But "the individual in its highest measure is beyond a man's power."[26] A man is only truly an individual, not in relation to other individuals or the crowd, but when he is alone before God, in relation to God. This theme draws us back to the process by which a man becomes aware of his ultimate individuality.

FEAR AND TREMBLING, INFINITE RESIGNATION, SUFFERING, CONSCIOUSNESS OF GUILT

By virtue of the suspension of the universal ethical demands which a man understands when he senses his unique and personal relation to God, the individual has moved into the religious sphere. He is in a state of sin, though unless he has moved into Religion B or the Christian religiousness he has not recognized the fact in its full implication; he is not conscious of his sin in all its seriousness. Kierkegaard calls the state of mind of the individual as he faces his unique relationship to God beyond the ethical stage "fear and trembling."[27] Within the first phase of religiousness the individual is released from realizing the ethical universal, in the Kantian or Hegelian sense, but now he has as his task "to exercise the absolute relation to the absolute telos, striving to reach the maxium of maintaining simultaneously a relation to the absolute telos and to relative ends, not by mediating them, but by making the relation to the absolute telos absolute and the relation to the relative ends relative."[28] This task of committing one's self absolutely to what is absolute and only relatively to one's various relative ends involves infinite resignation, suffering, and consciousness of guilt.

Infinite resignation is the negative counterpart of an individual's attempt to relate himself in an absolute way to the absolute. It is the renunciation of all relative ends, but this is an ideal task and, according to Kierkegaard, has probably never been achieved by anyone. It is one thing to renounce relative ends verbally, but it is quite another to express this existentially. The individual is in fact immersed in the immediate and in so far as this is true he is really committed absolutely to relative ends. It is because the individual is always to some degree immediate and thus absolutely committed to relative ends that ideally the movement of resignation is the renunciation of all relative ends. Such absolute renunciation is of course impossible, for existence itself stands in the way of man's constituting an absolute relationship from his own side.[29] The meaning of infinite resignation can thus be defined in terms of its direction—the absolute end—and its result—suffering. Kierkegaard deals with this theme of the necessity of an absolute relation to the absolute in more concrete ways. In *Purity of Heart*, for example, "willing one thing" is essentially the equivalent of having an absolute relation to the absolute; the barriers to willing one thing correspond to the relative ends which must be completely renounced. Or it is possible to characterize infinite resignation in terms of one's willingness to give up everything for the sake of one's eternal happiness. Where such willingness is present, one's whole existence is transformed absolutely. If there is anything one is not willing to give up, then the relationship to an eternal happiness is not present and the individual's inner life is not transformed.

The attempt to renounce relative ends under the conditions of finitude and temporality produces suffering, and suffering is one of the means by which self-awareness and self-development are intensified. To suffer personally and inwardly is not the same as knowing about suffering. There are those who suffer and there are those who become professors of the fact that others have suffered. Suffering does not simply come from the break with the immediate, but from the abyss within, which that attempted break discloses to us. Suffering signifies relation to one's self; it is a sign of inwardness, the distinctive mark of the religious sphere— of religious action. Action, however, is to be understood as inwardly directed. Action directed outward does not transform the individual's inner existence and hence remains in the aesthetic, not the religious, sphere. "Action in inwardness is suffering, for the individual cannot make himself over, any such attempt becoming, like imitation, a mere affectation, and it is for this reason that suffering is the highest action in inwardness."[30] Religious suffering is a dying away from immediacy, though this dying away is never once-for-all. It is persistent not only in the sense that it does not cease but also in the sense that it is present in the most highly de-

179

veloped religious individualities. The dying away to immediacy can also be stated as the principle that the individual can do absolutely nothing of himself, but is as nothing before God. Here self-annihilation is the essential form of the God-relationship. Just as resignation shows that the individual has the right orientation toward the absolute, so the persistence of the suffering shows that the individual remains in the correct position and preserves himself in it. Thus the religious man believes that it is precisely in suffering that life is to be found; one who lacks suffering lacks the religious. Not all suffering is a mark of the religious life. Religious suffering has a meaning—the meaning which has just been described; it is the suffering which emerges out of the conscious decision for the absolute. Without this decision one may suffer and suffer and go on suffering without such suffering having any meaning at all.

As long as one is absolutely related to the relative and yet seeks to renounce such a relationship, he will suffer. To be sure, this experience is a matter of degree, but at a certain point consciousness of guilt arises. The individual feels himself guilty because he is unable to accomplish his religious duty—an absolute relation to the absolute end. This guilt, moreover, is total guilt; it is not a matter of being guilty over this or that failure. Guilt becomes qualitative, Kierkegaard says, because the individual is confronted with the absolute quality in his relation to his eternal happiness.[31] Consciousness of guilt is the final intensification of self-awareness and self-development from within the self, but it is not the final step toward self-realization. The self does not yet see itself as it really is. Only when the self sees itself as a sinner alone before God with all that implies, when it sees itself separated from God by an infinite qualitative abyss, does it see itself as it really is. Only then, if an individual chooses or accepts himself, or better, knows himself for what he really is, does he receive by virtue of that act and God's grace a new self. This new self—this self in faith—is not something man can acquire by himself; it is the gift of God; it is the break with immanence, for man cannot know himself to be a sinner from within himself. God alone can show him that he is such.

DREAD, CONSCIOUSNESS OF SIN, THE PARADOX

How man becomes a sinner and how he comes to recognize himself as such, Kierkegaard develops at some length in his psychological study, *The Concept of Dread*. Since sin is the new existence medium and consciousness of sin represents the ultimate of self-awareness, it is important to examine Kierkegaard's interpretation of sin with some care. Sin is so decisive for Kierkegaard's understanding of the meaning of becoming a Christian because man can become a Christian only to the degree that he comes to know his own nature as a sinner. Consciousness of sin is decisive further because it is an alteration of the very subject himself. The other changes which have been described take place within the individual. This change is brought about from outside. For understanding Kierkegaard's views the discussion of sin in *The Concept of Dread* must be supplemented by his discussion of despair in *Sickness unto Death*.

That the consciousness of sin is the presupposition of ultimate self-realization is clearly stated by Kierkegaard at various points in his writings, but nowhere more clearly than in *Training in Christianity*, where, in speaking of the many ways in which Christ draws men unto himself, he writes: "all ways come together at one point, the consciousness of sin—through that passes 'the way' by which He draws a man, the repentant sinner, to Himself."[32] One does not become a Christian, or come to full personal existence, except through consciousness of sin. The most serious aspect of the consciousness of sin is not the becoming aware of one's particular sins, but the consciousness that one is "in sin," that he is a sinner. The consciousness of sin quite obviously presupposes sin, and sin, says Kierkegaard, presupposes itself. In short, sin is inexplicable. It is uncaused, or, to put it another way, sin arises out of freedom. Through sin, sinfulness came into the world. They entered the world together. In explaining his view, Kierkegaard relies partly on the biblical account of the Fall, interpreting the Fall in such a way that what happened to Adam is what happens to every man. Sin comes into the world anew with each individual. Sinfulness is not inherited except in the sense that an increment is passed along through the solidarity of the race. But Kierkegaard goes beyond the biblical account of the Fall in accounting for original sin when he says: "How sin came into the world every man understands by himself alone; if he would learn it from another he *eo ipso* misunderstands it."[33]

Yet if sin cannot be explained, in the sense that some necessary cause can be assigned to the entrance of sin into the world, still the psychological climate in which sin emerges can be described. The psychological climate in which sin emerges Kierkegaard calls "dread" or "anxiety." Dread or anxiety is one of the types of experience through which every individual must pass in the process of self-realization. In his Journals Kierkegaard writes: "Dread is the first reflex of possibility, a glimmer and yet a terrible spell."[34] Or again, it is "the reality of freedom as possibility anterior to possibility," it is a "sympathetic antipathy and an antipathetic sympathy."[35] Or one may liken it to dizziness, the "dizziness of freedom which occurs when the spirit would posit the synthesis, and freedom then gazes down into its own possibility, grasping at finiteness to sustain itself."[36] Sin comes into the world because under these circumstances freedom succumbs. The dizziness is not so much the cause as the occasion for sin.

A simpler statement of Kierkegaard's meaning would be that when an individual confronts his own freedom and the multiplicity of undetermined possibilities implied therein, he is both attracted and repelled. The combination of attraction and repulsion before one's own freedom, this ambivalence, is a kind of dizziness. It is out of this state or in this state that a man sins. It is in this state that he becomes a sinner. For Kierkegaard, anxiety is the intermediate determinate between possibility and actuality. It grows out of the consciousness of being able and carries with it the consciousness of selfhood. In other words, for Kierkegaard consciousness of freedom is consciousness of self. One might even say, the more self, the more freedom; the more freedom, the more self.

When sin enters the world, anxiety is compounded. "Sin enters by dread, but sin in turn brought dread with it."[37] Anxiety becomes more reflective; it is related to history and the historical nexus in which the individual finds himself, and various kinds of anxiety correspond to the components of the individual situation. There is the anxiety of shame felt in relation to one's sexuality and present in all erotic enjoyment; there is the anxiety of childbirth, etc. There is, in fact, a kind of anxiety corresponding in a general way to each of the spheres of existence. That of paganism is the anxiety which belongs to the aesthetic sphere. The anxiety of Judaism corresponds to the ethical sphere, while the anxiety of the Christian is religious anxiety. There is also anxiety before the evil, anxiety over the reality of sin, and anxiety over the future possibility of sin. Still another kind of anxiety is the dread of the good which Kierkegaard calls the "demoniacal." The demoniacal is an unfree relation to the good, toward freedom itself. Sin is posited, and the individual is anxious before possible freedom.

What specifically has anxiety to do with the realization of personal existence, with becoming a Christian? For Kierkegaard, anxiety intensifies self-awareness; by the aid of faith it is absolutely educative: "He who is educated by dread is educated by possibility, and only the man who is educated by possibility is educated in accordance with his infinity. Possibility is therefore the heaviest of all categories."[38] Dread is the saving experience by means of faith: "Only the man who has gone through the dread of possibility is educated to have no dread—not because he avoids the dreadful things of life, but because they always are weak in comparison with those of possibility."[39] And when "the individual is by possibility educated up to faith, dread will eradicate what it has itself produced."[40] The way is then paved for what Kierkegaard calls on other occasions "repetition." He will receive "everything back again, as in reality no one ever did even if he received everything double, for the pupil of possibility received infinity."[41]

In these and other passages Kierkegaard is saying that the

self that has been schooled in possibility has not only learned to face reality, but to face every possibility in the human situation. Such a person knows that he can demand absolutely nothing of life—that "terror, perdition, annihilation dwell next door."[42] Such a self faces the facts both about itself and its situation and is thereby free.[43] Only faith makes anxiety such a saving experience, for only faith gives the "courage to believe that the state of sin is itself a new sin" and courage "to renounce dread without any dread."[44] Not that faith annihilates dread but it overcomes the power of anxiety over life. Only faith is capable of doing this.

Both the anxiety which is the school of possibility leading to faith and the faith which overcomes this anxiety are to be understood in the context of the consciousness of sin. The consciousness of sin is the *conditio sine qua non* of becoming a Christian. It is this consciousness which binds a man to Christianity. If one is not convinced of his own sinful nature, Christianity becomes a scandal. Where there is consciousness of sin the individual is silenced. In spite of the possibility of offense he chooses faith. Consciousness of sin is related to despair in this: we only become fully conscious of our sin and its implications when we have been informed through revelation what sin is and then in despair and before God we will to be ourselves, or we will not to be ourselves, each one for himself individually.[45] This last movement in which man becomes conscious of himself as a sinner is made possible by the Paradox, the Christian affirmation that God became individual man in time. Man cannot make himself conscious of the meaning of his sin; only God can do that. In order to do this, God made himself an individual man so that man might understand. But the Incarnation is a contradiction. From the point of view of reason it is absurd that God, the Eternal, became man, individual man, in time. Such a notion is a paradox in that man cannot by means of thought resolve these opposites. In Religion A, God was thought of as immanent, as being in and through existence. Religion B represents the utmost heightening of the tension in human life. The Eternal is at one place and at one time. For Kierkegaard this is an Absolute Paradox. Thought rejects it; it is a scandal, an offense to the ordinary mind and to the speculative mind alike until one realizes that he is a sinner before God and that he needs the forgiveness offered by Christ. Then he believes that what the paradox asserts is true, and he believes it with his whole being, not just with his mind; in fact, he believes against his understanding. Against the absolute objection of reason, the individual, conscious of his sin, holds fast by the passion of inwardness to this objective uncertainty that God became an individual man in time. This is faith. The consciousness of sin individualizes, heightens the tension, sharpens man's subjectivity to the utmost. It is self-awareness moving to a climax. The recognition of his own situation moves man to that madness which is faith. It is the venture, the ultimate risk. The Christian must venture all, even his thought, believing against his understanding. Such existence as a man has under these conditions is personal existence; it is existence in faith, conceived not as a state, not as repose, or peace, but as continual struggle, persistent suffering. The tensions continue; there is no letup; sin continues even when there is consciousness of forgiveness. The struggle and the suffering of the Christian life Kierkegaard describes at length in works like *Training in*

Christianity, Works of Love, For Self-Examination, and *Judge for Yourselves!*

Sin consciousness and God consciousness come together through Revelation. We become conscious of sin in confronting the paradoxical self-disclosure of God. Kierkegaard writes of this in *Thoughts on Crucial Situations in Human Life* as the second wonder. Man's consciousness of God originally came through nature; it was the first wonder. Then despair took away man's wonder, and the second consciousness of God, the restoration of man's wonder, comes only through the Paradox. The wonder comes with the realization that what one seeks is given. Man becomes conscious of the depth of his own sin as he confronts the Paradox, and he is drawn into faith as his ultimate risk and ultimate hope as he sees himself for what he really is as he is alone before God. A life in faith is a new life; it is a break with immanence. Faith is not, however, a realm or a state. It is an existence medium, which is to say it is active, dynamic. "Faith is self-active in its relation to the improbable and the paradoxical, self-active in the discovery, and self-active in every moment holding it fast—in order to believe."[46] Faith is not an arbitrary act of man, like doubt; it is an objective act. There is in faith that which must presuppose the consciousness of sin, grace as well as choice, and there is choice only because there is grace. Faith is the highest sphere for the existing individual.

Such are the existence media of one who is becoming a Christian, of the movement toward authentic selfhood or true personal existence. It is a movement away from speculation and the aesthetic through despair, fear and trembling, dread, infinite resignation, suffering, consciousness of guilt to consciousness of sin and finally faith. But faith is no

187

stopping point. There is no rest, no peace within the world. There is only continuous struggle and suffering for the Christian. The movement from first to last is one of increasing tension, increasing inwardness, increasing subjectivity. Faith is the ultimate tension, for man becomes a new self by virtue of the historical revelation which is an offense to the understanding, an offense which is overcome only in opposition to the understanding.

Part of the richness of Kierkegaard's thought in describing how one becomes a Christian or realizes personal existence lies in the variety of approaches he makes to the subject and the interrelationship of these approaches. The movement which has been described in some detail is characterized by Kierkegaard in other ways. Personal existence or the process of becoming a Christian may also be understood as reduplication, as repetition, as a movement toward increasing inwardness and subjectivity, etc. Before turning to a consideration of the fundamental means by which one moves through the existence media to faith within the Christian life, it will be worthwhile examining several of these alternative modes of expression.

REDUPLICATION AND REPETITION

Reduplication is existential living; it is both a quality of existential thought and a quality of existential living taken as a whole. So far as thought is concerned, it is living in the categories of one's thought. Kierkegaard attacks Hegel and his contemporaries for failure in this regard. They do not live as their thought should imply. One hardly ever sees reduplication in this sense even in religious authors. Kierkegaard can think only of Augustine when he wants to mention a religious writer who lives in his own categories. If you look at two men, says Kierkegaard, you may find that one defends Christianity and the other attacks it; but, if you look at their lives, neither of them bothers too much about it. This is not reduplication; it is its opposite. Reduplication is being what one says; it is the opposite of pretending, of hypocrisy, of the double standard and the double life. It is transparency. Kierkegaard did not believe that real reduplication, real transparency is possible for a man considered autonomously. Genuine reduplication needs a third factor, a compelling external factor. This third factor is God; in fact, for Kierkegaard God is infinite reduplication, and it is only through God, in and through the Eternal, that reduplication is possible for man. Reduplication is the coincidence of the movement toward the interior and toward the exterior. When the eternal is present in a man, the movement outward and the movement inward correspond. By virtue of the eternal he is what he does and he does what he is; this is reduplication, relatively characteristic of man in moments of faith and infinitely characteristic of God eternally.

"Repetition" emphasizes another aspect of self-realization, or, perhaps better, it represents the summit of reduplication. Repetition is the consequence of faith; it is integration, the restoration of the self to unity and integrity. This restoration is really the gift of a new self. When man reaches the sphere of Christian faith he "receives everything back again."[47] Yet the everything he receives is not the finite everything which Kierkegaard seems to have been thinking of when he wrote *Fear and Trembling* or when he began to write the little work he calls *Repetition*. The repetition has to do with man's own self. One receives one's self again, not in its pristine integrity, but in such a manner as to make one doubly feel its significance.[48] The self which has had its innocence shattered and which has been brought back to its relationship to God by the hard road leading to faith is the same self, yet it is also true to say that it is a new self, infinitely richer. It is a new being—in Christ. Much more could be written of the significance of this concept and of the experience to which it refers in Kierkegaard's frame of thought, but it is perhaps sufficient to indicate that his interpretation of becoming a Christian can be subsumed under this category. Kierkegaard himself hints at this possibility when he has Constantin write: "Repetition is the *interest* of metaphysics, and at the same time the interest on which metaphysics suffers shipwreck; it is the solution of every ethical view of life; it is the *sine qua non* for every dogmatic position." And again: "Just as these [the Greeks] taught that all knowledge is recollection so the new philosophy will teach that the whole of life is repetition."[49] Of the term itself, Lowrie comments: "No term in S. K.'s vocabulary is more important."[50]

INWARDNESS AND PASSION—TOWARD INFINITE SUBJECTIVITY

Personal existence is not only reduplication and repetition; it may also be characterized as inwardness and the movement toward inwardness and the heightening of passion. Both movements are ways of increasing subjectivity. Or in terms of one's eternal happiness: "An eternal happiness inheres precisely in the recessive self-feeling of the subject, acquired through his utmost exertion."[51] Christianity assumes that there is in the subjectivity of the individual a potentiality for approximating eternal happiness. Christianity does not assume that the individual is immediately ready to accept eternal happiness or that he even knows its true significance. But the subject through infinite concentration on himself can be developed or transformed to constitute eternal happiness. In other words, the movement toward subjectivity, toward inwardness, is the movement toward eternal happiness. This is why Christianity may be described as the maximum expression of the principle that subjectivity, inwardness, is the truth. In fact, this is the first condition for becoming a Christian, to be absolutely turned inward, or, as Lowrie translates it, to be absolutely introverted.

Being thus infinitely introverted, the introvert has nothing whatever to do with anybody else—this is what it means to be serious. . . . Being thus introverted, the learner then understands, or learns to understand, what the task of becoming and being a Christian really is—every instant that he is extroverted is wasted, and if there are many such instants, all is lost.[52]

To be so introverted is to be alone before God with the Pattern (Christ) before one's eyes.

The rising tension of the increasing subjectivity and inwardness may be characterized in terms of the strong personal emotion or feeling involved. The movement of personal existence is a movement of rising passion. It is pathetic-dialectic. In its ultimate expression the pathos or feeling is infinite, heightened and reheightened by the dialectical crucifixion of the understanding in which the believer accepts the Absurd, the Paradox, in faith. Kierkegaard makes much of passion, and this emphasis on feeling is one of his positive relations to romanticism as well as the source of one of his critiques of rationalism. Passion is the culmination of existence for an existing individual, yet rationalistic philosophy is singularly unpassionate. Passion is expressed at every level of personal existence, but the more passion, the higher the level of personal existence. The more one is concerned with anything, the more passion. The more inwardly concerned with anything, the more passion, and when one is infinitely concerned in an inward direction passion rises to its height, only to be further intensified by the dialectical crucifixion of the understanding by means of the Paradox.

For Kierkegaard an infinite personal passionate interest is related to one's eternal happiness, and this in two ways. It is related in the first place because one realizes one's eternal happiness in expectation by means of the infinite passion which arises out of concern for it. In the second place, one's eternal happiness is itself a matter of infinite passion.

Christianity can be described in terms of passion as well as in terms of inwardness, for the infinite personal passion is a condition of faith. Faith is the highest passion, and faith is as near as we can get to our eternal happiness under the conditions of historical existence. "Christianity is spirit, spirit is inwardness, inwardness is subjectivity, subjectivity is essentially passion, and, in its maximum, an infinite, personal, passionate interest in one's eternal happiness."[53] In fact, only two kinds of people can know anything about Christianity—those who have an infinite passionate interest in their eternal happiness and those with an infinite passionate condemnation of Christianity. The speculative philosopher misses the whole meaning of Christianity because he turns it into something objective and dispassionate.

Passion is essential to the whole process of self-transcendence. One cannot transcend one's self objectively. The existential realization of a unity of finite and infinite which transcends existence comes only in the moment of passion. Self-realization through heightening of feeling is possible only because such intensity of feeling unifies the self. Passion is the temporal mode in which continuity is given to the life of the existing individual, and the phrase "to achieve continuity" is another way of expressing the nature of the process of becoming a Christian or attaining authentic personal existence. The difficulty facing the existing individual is how to give his existence continuity. An abstract continuity will not suffice; it is really no continuity at all. Passion gives the individual continuity, though this is only momentary and is both a restraining and a moving influence. Kierkegaard would go further; he would identify the eternal with the factor of continuity which emerges in infinite passion.

The eternal is the factor of continuity, but an abstract eternity is extraneous to the movement of life and a concrete eternity within the existing individual is the maximum degree of his passion. All idealizing passion is an anticipation of the eternal in existence functioning so as to help the individual to exist.[54]

Nor is passion passive; it is active, but the action is all inward. It involves the transformation of the entire existence of the individual. One must not simply have an idea of eternal happiness. The pathos consists in "transforming one's existence into a testimony concerning it."[55] This is the process of reduplication or achieving inner transparency. One may define eternal happiness only in terms of the mode of acquisition which involves maximum passion. Passion is not once-for-all; it is continuous, repeated, or it is worth nothing.

All the existence media might be called "passionate," for all of them, whether despair, consciousness of guilt, consciousness of sin, infinite resignation, suffering, anxiety, express with varying degrees of intensity the movement in concerned inwardness which is passion.

A NOTE ON VALUE

Commentators on Kierkegaard's thought have frequently pointed to the implicit philosophy of values in one or another of his works or in his work as a whole, and there can be little doubt that his approach to personal existence is qualitative and valuational. The various spheres of existence described throughout Kierkegaard's works are in fact a hierarchical value scheme, and within the spheres there is a similar hierarchy, though the distinctions are not so clear. Of course Kierkegaard's method is unusual; the valuations of life which form the subject matter are made to reveal themselves.[56] The categories of value are not and cannot be abstract. One does not live in logical, scientific, or metaphysical categories. Rather the categories are personal and concrete. The principle of putting values in an ascending scale is clear. This principle can be stated in a great variety of ways, all of which say essentially the same thing. Kierkegaard says that the highest value is freedom; therefore the more freedom, the more value.[57] Or Kierkegaard says that the highest good is love; therefore the more real love (as characterized in *Works of Love*), the more value.[58] Or again, the same thing can be said in terms of God as the highest good, or one's own immortality, or the eternal telos. Another way of coming at the same problem can be stated in terms of a scale of increasing subjectivity and inwardness. Using the framework of *Purity of Heart*, the scale would be based on the degree to which one is able to will one thing, i.e., the degree of unity and integration achieved. In this light the process leading to becoming a Christian or to authentic personal existence is one of realizing value on an ascending scale, reaching full actualization only as it approaches the highest good, be that good described as God, freedom, love, immortality, infinite subjectivity and inwardness, or the absolute telos. Such a philosophy of value is concrete, personal, existential. It is considerably different from many of our contemporary treatments of the problem of value.

Chapter 4

MAN OF PRAYER

Kierkegaard's interpretation of the process of becoming a Christian, of the movement toward authentic personal existence, is the fruit of his own experience and of the movement of his own life. So too is his understanding of the means by which the individual nourishes, sustains, and even endures this process in his own life. If faith is the goal, prayer is the means of moving toward that goal. From the beginning of his return to Christianity until his death Kierkegaard was a man of prayer. It is difficult to overestimate the significance of prayer for his life and thought. He came to think of prayer as man's "greatest earthly happiness."[1] Prayer was God's command.[2] One ought not to ask for reasons for praying; praying is like breathing– if you don't breathe, you die. If you don't pray, you die spiritually.[3] Prayer is man's means of renewing himself and reproducing his own spiritual vitality.

It is strange indeed how little attention scholars have given to the place of prayer in Kierkegaard's life and thought. One reason for this neglect has certainly been that interest has centered around his contribution to major issues in philosophical and theological discussion. Another is that those who have been interested in his life have centered their attention on its mysteries. They have tried to unearth his "secret" and to see through his mystification. Quite as important, however, has been Kierkegaard's own reticence regarding this intimate and deeply inward aspect of his life. Not only was he reserved about his own piety, but it was apparently easier for him to write of the more public aspects of the religious life such as faith or Christology than of that which was so private and personal as prayer. In 1849 he recorded that he prayed that he might be spared from having to speak openly of his own inwardness, his own relation to God, to say how he spent his time in prayer, how he really lived with God like father and son. This baring of himself he found "so difficult, so difficult"; "my inwardness," he wrote, "is too true for me to be able to talk about it."[4]

Reticent as Kierkegaard was in dealing with the meaning of prayer and its significance for his own life, at least in comparison with his handling of other themes, there is evidence enough both in his Journals and in his published works to support the assertion of the overarching significance of prayer for his life and thought. Two ways of substantiating this assertion lie before us: the first is to study Kierkegaard's practice of prayer and his reflections on his own prayer life; the other is to examine what he says about the nature and function of prayer in the religious life. Both approaches are interrelated.

KIERKEGAARD'S PIETY

There is an impressive continuity and stability in Kierkegaard's devotional life which a careful reader of the Journals will surely note. Apart from attendance at public worship until his break with the church, Kierkegaard devoted a definite time every day, "regularly and with monastic precision," to the reading of edifying books. He was brought up on Mynster's sermons, and he continued to read them. And he prayed. It might almost be said that prayer was his existence medium through all his adult life. Whatever his movement through the other existence media, whether he achieved faith himself or not, it is clear that he remained a man of prayer. The title of one of his edifying discourses, "The Righteous Man Strives in Prayer with God and Conquers in That God Conquers" might well be taken as the theme of his own life, though he understood the meaning of this theme differently as he moved more deeply into the Christian life.[5] Writing of the time immediately after his father's death when he had achieved financial independence and had no need of looking for a position, he commented: "How extraordinary that I should nevertheless have prayed every morning that God would give me strength for the work that Thou Thyself shouldst allot me."[6] Even before the great religious experience of May, 1838, he was struggling with himself in prayer. He wrote on the occasion of his visit to Rordams where he had met Regine for the first time: "Oh, God, how easily one forgets such resolutions. Once again I turned back to the world for some time, deposed in my inmost self, to dominate there. Oh, what does it help a man to win the whole world and injure his own soul."[7] And again: "Oh, how I feel that I am alone—Oh cursed be that arrogant satisfaction in standing alone—all will despise me now—but Thou, O my God, take not Thy hand from me now—let me live and better myself."[8]

Not long afterward Kierkegaard questioned himself, as he did more than once, as to whether his expressions of gratitude to God for what God had done for him arose out of fear of losing what he had received or out of a real religious certitude.[9] The year after his ecstatic religious experience he again reflected on his own prayer life, wondering whether he had been fully aware that God cannot be tempted: "Why do you lift up your voice, almost defiantly to heaven—why do your thoughts storm it, or do you think that your misfortune is so great, your complaint so justifiable, your sighs so deep and so moving, that God must be tempted by them?"[10] Again and again in the Journals he examined his own life of prayer; again and again he wrote of the occasions upon which he had resorted to prayer.

As might be expected the occasions especially noted by Kierkegaard as times for turning to God in prayer were critical ones in his life. Some of them were turning points. For example, when he most wanted to be a man of action, when he wanted to marry Regine, he found himself reduced to what "is usually left to women and children—to pray."[11] Later when he wished that he might at least let her know of his abiding love, he turned each such temptation into a prayer for her.[12] In the midst of his suffering over his broken engagement he prayed: "My Lord God, give me once more the courage to hope; merciful God let me hope once again, fructify my barren and infertile mind."[13]

Another turning point came as he sent the manuscript of the *Concluding Unscientific Postscript* to the printer. The completion of the manuscript, so he thought at the time, meant the end of his authorship. He was at a decisive point; he was considering holy orders—and he prayed. For several months he asked God's help in determining how he was to proceed. At about the same time he offered his challenge to the *Corsair*, and he wrote: "Two things in particular occupy me: (1) that whatever the cost I should remain intellectually true in the Greek sense to my life's idea; (2) that religiously it should be as ennobling as possible. For the second I pray to God."[14] And his further reflection on this occasion was: "The best help in all action is to pray; that is true genius; then one never goes wrong. . . ."[15] During the actual persecution by the *Corsair* he prayed: "God give me good fortune and help, and above all things spiritual certainty against the spiritual trials which come from within, for one can always fight against the world."[16] Finding himself made more and more ridiculous in the eyes of the common people, he reflected on his sympathy for them, thanked God for such sympathy as a gift of grace, and made it his "constant prayer" that his feeling for the suffering of the common folk might be preserved and increased even in the face of his growing separation from them.[17]

There were other occasions of stress which Kierkegaard particularly noted as occasions for prayer. In the midst of his worries over the publication of *Sickness unto Death* he turned to God and prayed that God might educate him, that he might learn in the tension of reality how far he was to go.[18] When he felt that God was leading him to a kind of resolution after he had preached one Sunday in the Citadel Church, he prayed that something new might be born in him. As he looked back upon this experience, he saw that God had educated him and had brought something new to birth in him. He had come to understand his relation to Christianity in a new way; he had gained new insight into how far God wanted him to go.[19]

Sometimes Kierkegaard prayed for specific individuals. His prayers for Regine have already been mentioned. Another example is related to Rasmus Nielsen. Nielsen was a professor of philosophy whom Kierkegaard had taken on as a kind of associate so that someone might one day carry on and interpret a work which Kierkegaard himself felt was drawing to a close. This relationship had not been a happy one, and Kierkegaard's irritation with Nielsen was increasing. In August, 1848, he wrote: "I had stopped praying for Rasmus Nielsen because I had been a little impatient with him, but which I felt to be such a dreadful sin against him that I immediately brought him back again into my relation to God."[20]

Toward the end of what had been his lifelong struggle with his melancholy, as he reflected on what seemed to him to be a growing deliverance from its power, Kierkegaard broke into a prayer of thanksgiving and joy: "O depths of the riches of God, Oh, how unsearchable are Thy ways, O God, but in all things fatherly and grace-giving."[21] Similar effusions are to be found in the midst of Kierkegaard's many reflections on the state of his inward life and in his examination of the transformations which his own prayer had undergone. Doubtless everything that Kierkegaard wrote about prayer bears some relation to his own inwardness, but those passages in which he reviews his experience of prayer reveal in a special way the intimacy of his relation to God, an intimacy which lies hidden in mystery in many of his other works. These moments of self-examination provide another important clue for establishing the place of prayer in Kierkegaard's life and thought.

As he considered his own experience in praying, he came to feel that prayer was exceedingly difficult. It seemed easy enough perhaps to one who had never prayed, or never really prayed. To pray, to know how to pray, becomes more and more difficult the more one prays. The more one understands what he is trying to do—to have a relationship with God—the more presumptuous this appears to be. In fact, according to Kierkegaard, if man had not been commanded by God to pray, he might well give it up. The more one comes to realize the difficulty of prayer, the more one realizes that in a sense the only real prayer is that one might be enabled to pray; then prayer becomes a silent surrendering of everything to God. In just the same way it may look easy to one who never prays or who prays by rote to bring prayer to its conclusion. For one who truly struggles in prayer, however, there always seems to be something more upon his heart. One must become transparent before God in all one's weakness and hope, but this is difficult indeed. This resolution of faith is hard, and yet when one has prayed to exhaustion as one can weep to exhaustion, then there is only one thing more: Amen. Rare as Kierkegaard felt this experience to be, he came to it in his own life. Speaking of his own experience, he wrote: "I almost feel the urge to say no single word more except this: Amen; for my gratitude to Providence for what It has done for me, overwhelms me . . . but thus even, through the unspeakable grace and help of God have I become myself."[22]

That his gratitude was not a momentary thing Kierkegaard made clear in the following passage:

It is wonderful how God's love overwhelms me—alas, ultimately I know of no truer prayer than what I pray over and over again, that God will allow me and not be angry with me because I continuously thank him for having done and for doing, yes, and for doing so indescribably much more for me than I ever expected.[23]

Whatever Kierkegaard came to write of the infinite qualitative difference between man and God, the infinite distance which separates them, his way of expressing his own God-relationship through prayer seems to speak a very different language. His relationship to God in prayer is like that of a father and a son. It was this relationship about which he was so reticent. The theme of being related to God as son to father recurs in his writings. It forms the substance of the way in which he understood his own God-relationship. "I have absolutely lived with God as one lives with a father. Amen."[24] He learned the meaning of divine fatherly love from his experience of his own father's love, and this notion became "the one unshakeable thing in life, the true archimedean point."[25] Writing in deeply personal terms of his experience of prayer before God, Kierkegaard stated: "He lets me weep before him in silent solitude, pour forth and again pour forth my pain, with the blessed consolation of knowing that he is concerned for me—and in the meanwhile he gives that life of pain a significance which almost overwhelms me. . . ."[26]

In 1852 as he reviewed his own Christian progress Kierkegaard felt that he had returned to the same point he had reached four years earlier but with a higher understanding. He was no longer concerned with the intellectual problem of the meaning of Christianity. Now he bore a new and direct relationship to the Christian faith. He saw himself called as a witness; he was to "suffer for the doctrine." He wrote: "It is the imitation of Christ that must now be introduced and I must be what I am, in being different from others." Such thoughts moved him to prayer:

O my God, it was Thou who didst hold Thy hand over me so that in the long hours of anguish I should not go and take a step in the direction of becoming like others and thereby become guilty of procuring an abortion. . . .

O my God, how clearly it now all stands out before me, how endlessly much has already been done for me. It is not difference that I must pray myself out of; that is not the task, but alas I shall never know security, which consists in being like others. No, I remain with Thee—and verily I know its happiness. . . .[27]

Passages like these illustrate the part which the practice of prayer played in Kierkegaard's life. They may also seem to substantiate the claim made by Karl Jaspers that Kierkegaard's was really a simple straightforward piety as distinguished from the tormented and complex nature of his thought. The expressions of assurance of God's love, the description of his relationship to God as that of a son to a father, the absence of skepticism or doubt within the life of prayer—these would seem to support Jaspers' point of view.[28] There is a considerable degree of truth in such a contention, for his experience at prayer was a kind of gyroscope or balance wheel of his spiritual life, and his prayer was rooted in a fundamental trust in God, come what may. Yet it would be a mistake to rest the interpretation here. The more deeply Kierkegaard moved into the Christian life, the more his own piety reflected the complexity of his interpretation of that life. The problem of the existential meaning of the Christian life, the implications of the infinite qualitative difference between man and God, the understanding of the depth of man's sin are all reflected in Kierkegaard's experience and understanding of his own devotional life.

Toward the end of his life he reflected on the transformation both in his conception of prayer and in the way he himself prayed. The passages in his Journal for 1853 containing these reflections represent his mature view of prayer. They are worth quoting at length both as an introduction to a discussion of Kierkegaard's understanding of the nature and function of prayer and also as a further indication that his piety was not quite so simple as Jaspers would have it.

There was a time—it came so naturally, it was childlike—when I believed that God's love also expressed itself by sending earthly "good gifts," happiness, prosperity. How foolhardy my soul was in desiring, and daring—for this is how I thought of it: One must not make the all-powerful petty; I prayed for everything, even the most foolhardy things, yet one thing excepted, exemption from the deep suffering beneath which I have suffered from my earliest days, but which I understood as belonging to my relation to God. But as for the rest, I should have dared anything. And when (for the suffering was simply the exceptional) everything succeeded, how rich my soul was in thankfulness, so happy in giving thanks—for I was convinced that God's love could express itself by sending the good gifts of the earth.

Now it is otherwise. How did that happen? Quite simply, but little by little. Little by little, I noticed increasingly that all those whom God really loved, the examples, etc., had all had to suffer in this world. Furthermore, that that is the teaching of Christianity: to be loved by God and to love God is to suffer. But if that were so then I dared not pray for good fortune and success because it was as though I were to beg at the same time: Will you not, O God, cease loving me and allow me to stop loving you. When a desire awoke in me—and I wished to pray, all my former burning inwardness was blown away; for it was as though God looked upon me and said: "Little child, think carefully what you are doing, do you wish me not to love you, and do you wish to be excused from loving me?"

On the other hand, to pray directly for suffering appeared to me too exalted, and it also seemed to me that it might easily be presumptuous, and that God might grow angry at my perhaps wishing to defy him.

For a long time my prayer has therefore been different; it really is a silent surrendering of everything to God because it is not quite plain to me how I should pray.[29]

And as he adds a bit later in the Journals: "As I have remarked earlier in this Journal: I have stopped at this difficulty, my prayer is not as it was earlier, but it is more of a tranquil abandonment to God, that it must become clear to me what place grace is to have."[30]

KIERKEGAARD'S INTERPRETATION OF PRAYER

Not only is prayer man's greatest earthly happiness according to Kierkegaard; it is the daughter of faith—the daughter whose task it is to nourish and sustain the mother.[31] Prayer is the means by which one comes to "will one thing."[32] It is the entrance gate into the Kingdom of God. But coming to will one thing or entering the gate to the Kingdom is neither easy nor simple. Jaspers' implication that Kierkegaard's was a simple piety is no more sustained by a consideration of his interpretation of prayer than it was by the consideration of his personal prayer life. Just as faith is immediacy *after* reflection, not simple immediacy, so too prayer, while it ends in a childlike trust in a fatherly God, in an absolute self-surrender based upon an absolute confidence, does not begin there. The root of true prayer for Kierkegaard, like the root of all Christian piety, is the sense of one's own unworthiness.[33] Kierkegaard's view of prayer is governed by what might be called a reality principle. What is man in comparison with God? Because man is a sinner there is an infinite qualitative difference between him and God. In effect, this means that man is nothing as he confronts the high and holy One. True prayer begins and moves through this recognition—this seeing one's self as he really is when he is alone before God. The movement of prayer is dialectical. From the sense of one's own unworthiness one moves to an understanding of the absolute distance between himself and God and then even while maintaining this sense of distance in unresolved tension one comes to understand through one's whole being that he is accepted by God even though he is unacceptable. Christian prayer begins with this heightened sense of one's own individuality. The task in prayer is to detach one's self from social ties and social dependence and come alone before God.[34] Prayer has solitude for its mother as well as faith.[35] As one becomes more and more aware of what God is, his own sense of unworthiness and sin becomes greater and greater. The relation rises in tension as the individual attempts to think of God in each moment. The more he detaches himself from social dependencies in this relation to God, the more he learns how to maintain the thought of God each moment within himself. The thought of God is rooted in a need for God, and the thought of God in each moment is a consciousness of the need of God in each moment. The ever present danger in this process rests at two points. The individual may become discouraged and give up. The more he humbles himself and the higher God becomes, the more he may be filled by fear and dread. God may become so fantastically elevated in his thought that the relationship is volatilized or his own ideality may be such that he gives up. He asks himself how he can pray. What can prayer mean to such an One? At this point prayer must not be given up. Such a temptation must be combated, Kierkegaard says. One must thank God for having commanded man to pray, for having made it a duty.

And he must go farther. He must confront himself with the fact that this Infinite One to whom he prays is also love, that he is a God of patience and consolation. God's love is not like man's love. Such a comparison would be a caricature. God is *Infinite* Love. The man of prayer must remember that God disposes at each instant of unnumbered possibilities. What he does at each moment is for the best, even if the one who prays cannot now understand this fact. What is demanded is frank courage and childlike trust. Only a childlike soul can truly adore God or express the love which loves God without reserve. ". . . let one only close his eyes, just think of God, be a poor solitary person whom God's infinite love gives the free courage of a child, other than that rejoice at the thought that thus every man has a right, yea, an obligation so to do."[36] It is the child's inwardness and trust that are to be emulated, not his prayer or his piety, for the child has an inadequate understanding of God and a childish conception of what is good.

What is necessary is absolute trust, absolute openness, absolute sincerity. We should even ask God with all the sincerity that we possess that we might not falsely and unconsciously hide anything from him. The task is to become transparent before God in all our weakness and all our hope.[37] There must be no holding back; no willingness to commit one's self only up to a certain point. Nor can one hold some aspect of his being outside the prayer relationship. Kierkegaard points out the incongruity of a scientist who prays and yet strives to prove the existence of God. "How is he able to pray from the depths of his heart when his being is divided in this contradiction?"[38] Prayer is unconditional surrender. All our relative purposes must be extinguished;

yet at the same time in our prayer we must acknowledge and confess the presumption that lies within such an attempt.[39]

What is called for is absolute self-surrender. The rising consciousness of self in the God-relationship brings with it the increasing willingness to surrender one's self, for it is paralleled by a deepening awareness of the greatness of God, that man is nothing without him, and that he is all in all. Prayer thus becomes the relationship in which self-will is progressively surrendered and God's will becomes the focus of the individual's life.[40] The individual no longer prays that his will be done, that his little purposes be served, or even that his own enterprises succeed in a worldly sense. He prays rather for God's blessing on his undertaking.[41] Such a prayer means that he consecrates himself and what he hopes to undertake to God's service—whether it succeeds or no. The blessing he desires is the blessing on the prayer itself—that the undertaking or the prayer for the undertaking might be such that God would bless it. In this the individual renounces himself. He surrenders all to God and accepts all from God. He prays for God's grace. Such a prayer means that he does not ask God to help him in any other way than as God himself wills. It means too that whatever happens he accepts as from the hands of God.

Prayer is thus a struggle in which man conquers in that God conquers. Man conquers in the sense that only if God conquers can man become the self which he was created to be; only so can he find fulfilment or be fulfilled.[42] In prayer man yields; God increases; man decreases. This is the law of all true love, says Kierkegaard. By yielding, by decreasing, one does not lose anything except his egoism. If one desired things otherwise, if he desired to increase while God increased—that would be self-love. Perfect happiness can only come through this prayer and its fulfilment: "He must increase, but I must decrease."[43]

In such prayer everything comes to be referred to God. Like Job, the man of prayer must come to see everything, both prosperity and adversity, as the gift of God. All things work together for good to them that love God, even though one may not be able to understand how this may be. When man is able to take this position in prayer, when in self-denial or self-abnegation man comes to comprehend his own nothingness, to see himself as he really is (to fail to do this is to lose one's soul), then the one who prays is himself changed. He is transformed. In the inwardness of prayer God becomes an end, not a means. The individual even prays that God should help him against himself, that even against his own will God's will for him might be done. Such a prayer means a putting away of all self-concern, casting out all desires and wishes other than this. It is willing one thing. To will one thing, to get rid of all personal desires is to put one's self-concern, one's selfishness, in God's hands. It is to become nothing. When this happens, the moment of transformation has come. Only when the one who prays has become nothing, "only then can God shine through him so that he resembles God. However great he is, he cannot express this resemblance to God. God can only imprint Himself upon him when he has himself become nothing."[44] Such transformation made possible through prayer is a transfiguration, a transfiguration in God. It consists in this, "that he reflects God's image."

So prayer might be understood within the categories of

immanence and so it is to be understood within Christian categories, but with one difference. If the man of prayer is a Christian, he realizes that such prayer and such transformation are not simple possibilities. They are not a possibility for him as a natural man. It is Christ who makes them possibilities for him. It is Christ who makes man conscious of his sinful state; it is Christ who is man's assurance that God is Infinite Love. The Christian can pray, can come to see himself as he really is and be related to God as God really is because in Christ his sin stands forgiven; in Christ his sin is forgotten. The Christian who prays is a penitent; he realizes with utmost inwardness that he is forgiven; that his prayer can be sustained only because satisfaction has been made.[45]

The God to whom we pray is infinitely distant from us because of our sin. We become aware of this as we become increasingly aware of the infinite seriousness of our sinfulness. Yet at the same time, because of Christ, we know that the God to whom we pray is closer to us than any human being. In prayer we grasp this existentially; in childlike trust we believe: we believe that he is Infinite Love. The crucial thing is not that such a belief is a generally accepted article of the Christian religion, not that *we* believe, but that *I* believe.[46] It is thus that one reaches religious reality. Then God is able to intervene. God is both infinitely distant and infinitely near.

Because God is infinitely near, because prayer is a relationship which isolates from others and draws the person praying closer to him, God can become the individual's unique confidante. One can live with him as Kierkegaard did, as a son with his father. The individual can open himself up to him, can seek him day and night in intimacy. Such a relationship can be maintained only in solitude. One cannot depend on others. He must come alone before God. Even public prayer becomes true prayer only as the *individual* opens himself to God and as he listens to the prayer. He must pray silently with his own heart in and through the words of the public prayer.[47]

For all the intimacy with God possible in the prayer relationship, prayer can be undertaken only in fear and trembling. To pray is a terribly serious act; it puts one under infinite obligation.[48] A prayer for help obligates us to accept that help in whatever form it comes. A rash prayer is a dangerous thing. One must not enter into prayer unadvisedly or lightly, but reverently, discreetly, advisedly, soberly, and in the fear of God. One will do so only if he has full realization of what prayer means and to whom he directs his prayer. Prayer in the name of Christ is equally fearful, for such prayer carries with it the obligation of imitation. Prayers made in the name of Christ obligate one to suffering, to privations so great that the one who prays really dies to the world.[49] Such prayers mean also that what one prays for is fit to be coupled with his name. To pray in the name of Jesus is

to pray in such a way that it is in conformity with the will of Jesus. I cannot pray in the name of Jesus to have my own will; the name of Jesus is not a signature of no importance, but the decisive factor; the fact that the name of Jesus Christ comes at the beginning is not prayer in the name of Jesus; but it means to pray in such a manner that I dare name Jesus in it; that is to say think of him, think of his holy will together with what I am praying for . . . it means . . . [that] Jesus assumes the responsibility and all the consequences, he steps forward for us, steps into the place of the person praying.[50]

In the deepest sense prayer is the human language.[51] In comparison with the Christian who prays, the heathen, no matter how much or how profoundly he speaks, is dumb. All other language is something less than the full expression of man's humanity. The language of prayer is the language of openness, and, understood in its deepest sense, the language of openness to God is silence. Silence means forgetting one's self, forgetting one's own plans for life and the future. It means forgetting one's own name whether that name be a great name or an insignificant name. It means forgetting one's own will and losing all one's wilfulness. In place of self it puts God. In place of one's own name it puts God's name. In place of one's own will it puts God's will. Hallowed be *Thy* name. *Thy* Kingdom come. *Thy* will be done.[52] To learn how to pray is to learn how to keep silence before him. The man of prayer learns this in and through the act of praying. Kierkegaard describes how this may happen:

There was something which lay so close to his heart, a matter of so much consequence to him, it was so important that he should make God understand him, he was afraid that in this prayer he might forget something; ah, and if he had forgotten it, he was afraid that God might not Himself remember it— therefore he would collect himself and pray indeed right earnestly. The surprising thing happened to him. In proportion as he became more and more earnest in prayer, he had less and less to say, and in the end he became quite silent.[53]

Man begins by thinking that to pray is to speak, to be heard, but he comes finally to realize that true prayer is to remain silent, to wait until he hears God:

The immediate person thinks and imagines that when he prays, the important thing, the thing he must concentrate upon, is that

God should hear what *he is praying for.* And yet in the true eternal sense it is just the reverse: the true relation in prayer is not when God hears what is prayed for, but when *the person praying* continues to pray until he is *the one who hears, who hears what God wills.* The immediate person, therefore, uses many words and, therefore, makes demands in his prayer; the true man of prayer only *attends.*[54]

Prayer does not always begin with silence, but true prayer always ends by becoming silence. Such silence is the key to the basic Christian goal—seeking the Kingdom first. To seek the Kingdom first is to eliminate all other possibilities and to pray, and true prayer means to become silent before God. This is what it means to seek first God's Kingdom.[55]

Prayer, even the best or truest prayer, does not change God, for God is unchangeable. A natural reaction might be then to question the efficacy of prayer. Prayer does not "work" on earth. It sows in what changes, but it reaps in what does not change. Its efficacy lies in what it makes possible for the one who prays. Prayer does not change God; it changes man. Prayer makes possible the inner transformation of the one who prays. It is only superstition, says Kierkegaard, to believe that God acts on man in an external way.[56] God is spirit. He acts inwardly—upon the inner man. There is no use in thinking that we tell God something he does not know when we pray, for he is all-knowing. A prayer of confession does not help God to know the one who confesses. Rather, "the maker of the confession gets to know about himself." Prayer is thus a means of self-understanding, the kind of self-understanding which can lead to self-realization or self-actualization, a realization or an actualization not wrought by the self but by God. Prayer is what we do so that God can do something to us and with us. It prepares the way for God; by opening ourselves to God in prayer, we make it possible for him to enter in and transform us. We keep a great deal about ourselves hidden from others below the surface; nor do we have complete self-understanding. When we open ourselves to God, we pave the way for new self-understanding. Prayer is thus a means of getting rid of some of our own ignorance about ourselves. Prayer is the means of attaining purity of heart, of overcoming our doublemindedness and self-deception, of ridding ourselves of the deceptive ignorance about ourselves which hides the darker side of our inward lives. In modern language we might say that prayer is the means of dredging our unconscious, of bringing to light what we did not know was in us. The hate, the anger, the despondency, our fear, our despair, our pride and envy, our self-trust—all these and more can be in prayer drawn out into the open so that we come to see ourselves as we really are.[57]

Is Kierkegaard's point then that the efficacy of prayer lies in the promotion of mental health? No, such a conclusion would be based upon misunderstanding. Prayer is what a man does so that God can do something with him. God can do nothing with him until man sees himself as he really is. Prayer is the means by which and the medium in which man gains this self-knowledge and becomes "teachable." It is the means by which a man becomes "existent for God" and God becomes existent for him, or available to him as he becomes open to God. Kierkegaard draws an analogy. Just as the rain falls on the just and the unjust but is beneficial only where the ground is fertile and cultivated, so the benediction of the Spirit is ever available, but it is beneficial only when a man kneels alone before God in prayer. Prayer is the means by which man gets his own ground ready.[58]

Thus prayer is not useless, though God does nòt change. Prayer is rather the most important thing of all.[59] There is no prospect of becoming a Christian or of eternal happiness if a man will not pray or learn how to pray truly. The unchangeability of God must be properly understood, however. God's unchangeability is his faithfulness and his love. He is infinitely available because he is unchangeable. No matter what man does, God is faithful in his relationship to man. "He abideth faithful."[60] Man's understanding of God's faithfulness is limited. At a given time he may not be able to comprehend God's fidelity, yet as Kierkegaard found again and again in his own life, God remains faithful. His love is unchanging; he is always available; he acts in and through all that happens to a man. In relation to man God's faithfulness may lie hidden in what appears to be or actually is a deceit. For Kierkegaard, as for Luther and Savonarola, even this deceit is not a sign of changeability or faithlessness. Rather every man who enters into a true relationship with God comes to a time when he is obliged to cry: "Thou hast deceived me, O God, but for my own good. Thou hast deceived me, O God, but in order to introduce me to the truth."[61] In the face of such understanding man should remember that God is eternally the same, that he has eternally the same loving care for edifying us. The one who comes closest to the truth, who best praises God, is the one who simply invokes God's faithfulness or who perhaps cries: "Thou faithful One, Thou hast deceived me into the truth. Thou wert too gracious and too faithful not to deceive me so that I lived on in an imagined conception of Thy faith-

fulness, but never entered into relationship with Thee."[62]
This view of God's unchangeability and faithfulness is
directly related to Kierkegaard's understanding of the relation of God and prayer to Christian suffering. No matter
how the case seems to appear from the standpoint of human
judgment, of human ideas of good and evil, of the agreeable
and the disagreeable, one must understand that all that God
does is good and learn to thank him.[63] Again and again
Kierkegaard comes back to the reflection that prayer ought
not to be directed toward the "good things" as man understands them, nor must man take the presence of such things
in his life as a sign of God's special goodness to him and therefore utter words of thanksgiving. No, we are to be thankful
whatever God gives us, for all that God does is good and for
a man's best interest, even what the men themselves from a
purely human standpoint might judge otherwise or be
unable to comprehend. That Kierkegaard was speaking out
of his own experience becomes clear when we see how many
times he recorded in his Journals his inability to comprehend
at one time that which only later he came to understand as
an expression of God's providence and special care for him.
His position in this regard is perhaps most intensely revealed
in his discussions of the relation of prayer to suffering.

However repugnant suffering may be from the purely
human standpoint, for the Christian suffering for the truth
or because one is a witness to the truth must be understood
as a sign of a true God-relationship. Relationship to God implies suffering.[64] "The nearer to Thee, the more pain,"
Kierkegaard wrote.[65] The more one enters into a relation to
God, the more misery and suffering one has. The true
Christian doctrine is that suffering alone is inevitable. It is

impossible to enter into a relationship with God, to be truly religious, without bearing the mark of a wound received. Such suffering is a sign that we are in true relationship. When everything goes against you, and yet you perceive in your inner consciousness a witness assuring you that you are on the right way, this is to be taken as a testimony of the spirit. In such suffering prayer is man's consolation. Ordinarily prayer is thought of as a consolation in relation to suffering because men pray to be relieved of the suffering. For Kierkegaard it is otherwise. The consolation which is available to a witness for the truth is that of being able to ask God to strengthen him in order to bear all suffering. "Thus by prayer he digs down always more to the heart of suffering; the nearer he approaches God in intimacy, the more he anchors himself in suffering." The one who is a witness for the truth sees before him a life full of suffering which is going to increase to the end, and he asks God for the strength to bear it. Each time he prays in this way, he strengthens himself, and anchors himself in the conviction that he will know how to sustain suffering.[66] Does this mean that a Christian should pray for suffering?[67] No, to desire suffering would be a temptation. If one suffers, one should pray that he may be able to bear the suffering. If one does not suffer and yet he prays for help in becoming a Christian, or that he may truly adore God, or that he may imitate Christ, or perhaps that God should educate him, he should realize that all these will entail suffering. The New Testament teaches, according to Kierkegaard, that a triumph in the world, an escape from suffering, is a sign that God has not helped a man. "The pagan does not want to suffer at all; the Jew may want to endure suffering for a few years, but still wants to triumph in this world and to enjoy this life. The Christian wishes to suffer his whole life long."[68] But the New Testament teaches that a spirit will be sent to him which will make him happy in his suffering. The suffering of infinite resignation, of dying to the world, are taken up in truly Christian suffering in the meaning of the phrase "dying to self." To pray for education, as Kierkegaard himself frequently did, implies, when a man finally comes to understand it, education through suffering.

And yet in all of this, for the Christian his suffering comes to be his greatest joy, for in a sense it is the guaranty of his God-relationship, and then a man will come to thank God, even as Kierkegaard himself did, for this gift of suffering. So Kierkegaard can write of the man who asked God to educate him and to whom God brings suffering:

At last our man gets completely tired, breaks down—and behold, just then the metamorphosis is produced and he cries out: "O, Thou my God, Thanks, O thanks; I see that I had forgotten that I had prayed that Thou wouldst educate me Thyself. Alas, as long as things were at their worst, I could not think or remember how it was to understand, O, but now I remember it again."[69]

In the profoundest sense, Kierkegaard says, this is what happens to every man who enters truly into a relationship with God. This is what had happened to him, for in the Journals we find him repeatedly thanking God for what he has had to suffer, expressing indescribable joy and happiness in his suffering. Such joy is possible not only because this suffering is a kind of guaranty of the God-relationship but also because it is an expression or proof of God's infinite love. One learns through prayer that God cares and loves him, no matter what. Even more than this, one knows that God shares this suffering: "I know that in Thy love Thou sufferest with me more than I, Infinite Love. Although Thou art not able to be changed for that."[70] One knows that God knows him, loves him, and cares for him, come what may.

Prayer, then, can even turn suffering into joy for a Christian. Prayer can give him the patience to bear the suffering. It can also remind him that a man only suffers once. It does this by reminding him every day of what alone is worth living for, that however long we suffer temporally it is but once, since the Christian's triumph through such suffering is for eternity.[71] True prayer even in the midst of suffering culminates in joy, for as in the model of all true prayer, it "prays itself joyful, and more joyful, and absolutely joyful." At last there is nothing, nothing whatever more to pray for or desire, and so with absolute joyfulness it concludes:

For thine is the kingdom and the power and the glory. Yes, His is the Kingdom; and therefore thou art to be absolutely silent, lest thou might make it disturbingly noticeable that thou dost exist, but that with absolute silence thou mayest express the fact that the kingdom is His. And His is the power; and therefore thou art to be absolutely obedient and art with absolute obedience to bear with everything, for His is the power. And His is the glory; therefore in all that thou doest and in all that thou endurest, thou hast absolutely one thing more to do; to give Him the glory, for the glory is His.[72]

This is truly a prayer of joy because it reminds us as often as we pray it that we not only do not and cannot depend on ourselves but that we need not depend on ourselves. It is a reminder that the One who surrounds us with his infinite love possesses the Kingdom and the power and the glory. It is the joy of the assurance that everything is possible for God, for the One who is love, or that the One to whom all is possible is love. It is the assurance that all things work together for good to them who love God. Is not this a great joy, sustained by the certitude that man can express his love to God in prayer? "That you are able at every moment to close your door and speak to God without an intermediary, without having to pay a heavy charge to appear before a great one, is this not a happiness?"[73] Is it not a great joy that prayer is our defense against the power of anxiety?[74] Is not the command to pray the assurance that nothing can separate the one who prays from the love of Christ? Is it not the joy of knowing the way to a place—a place of prayer—where God makes himself available to man?[75] Is it not the joy of finding what Kierkegaard himself was seeking from the beginning, that Archimedean point outside the world—an oratory where a man really prays in all sincerity—from which to move the earth?[76]

Such a positive and powerful view of the nature and function of prayer in the Christian life contains within itself a critique of false and inadequate prayer. Kierkegaard's view of true prayer implies a concept of false prayer. There is, for example, no true prayer without suffering. False prayer asks relief from suffering. True prayer asks the strength to bear it. False prayer falsely conceives of God. It thinks God is changeable; it tempts God, but God neither tempts nor can be tempted. It thinks God operates in terms of human conceptions of good and evil, pleasant and unpleasant. It turns God into man writ large, as if he could be persuaded, cajoled, bargained with. True prayer is patient and persistent. False prayer is halting and impatient. The individual who prays truly is humble and finds the experience of prayer humbling. The individual who prays falsely bolsters his own self-esteem and is presumptuous in his prayer. True prayer accepts everything and refers everything to God. The one who prays falsely complains and then gives thanks only for what he himself thinks is good. The true man of prayer is totally committed. His opposite holds something back, or he prays with only a part of his being—his mind, his feelings, or his public self. In valid prayer a man comes alone before God. In immature prayer the individual tries to maintain his dependencies on his fellow man and his social world as a kind of protective device. True prayer maintains the dialectical tension in man's sense of the distance and the nearness of God; false prayer either volatilizes the God-relationship in a fantastically elevated conception of God or so likens God to man that it treats God as a fellow human being. The man who prays truly strips himself of all cleverness, while false prayer is often an attempt at clever conversation "pumped out by an excavating reflection."[77] The man who truly prays listens to God; the man who prays falsely wants God to listen to him.

Learning by heart certain formulas because they have been used by others with success is still another false way of praying.[78] It is a means of fostering dependence on others. Equally to be condemned is the dependence on certain hours for meditation. Christianity is the faith which is at the center of reality every moment, every day of the week. Those who reduce it to "hours of meditation" proclaim thereby that they are not Christians. It is hypocritical; it puts Christianity at a distance.[79] It is, says Kierkegaard, a kind of adoration like that of those who adore God by having their Bibles rebound in velour or who construct marble temples in which everything is of gold.[80] Long and prolix prayers are dangerous too. They may conceal a kind of unbelief or degenerate into temporization to the detriment of action. On the other hand, they may defeat true prayer by keeping before one what he really ought to forget. For example if one's mind is filled with evil thoughts, the best prayer is not to linger over these as a problem. The longer and more fearful such a prayer becomes the more one cultivates the evil thoughts he would be rid of. In this case one must "learn to acquire in all haste the most intensive trust in God. There is not time to add another word to the prayer, for then I am reminded of what I should forget. Here the prayer is a tacit accord with God, expressing confidence in Him."[81]

Most of all one's prayer should express one's total dependence upon God. All true prayer is grounded in this dependence, for it is the Holy Spirit who works in prayer in such a fashion that the only real prayer is that of being able to pray. Man alone can acknowledge this, do it, and desire it.[82] So Kierkegaard himself learned to live, and so he learned to die. On his deathbed he was asked by his friend Emil Boesen whether he could pray in peace to God:

Yes, that I can; first of all I pray that my sins may be forgiven me, that everything may be forgiven; then I pray that I may be free from despair in death, and the words often occur to me where it is said that death should be pleasing to God; and so I pray for what I so much desire, which is that I may know a little beforehand when death is to come.[83]

So Kierkegaard had lived, so he died—a man of prayer.

Notes

NOTES

References to Kierkegaard's works in English translation are abbreviated; full bibliographical data and titles are given following the notes. References to the Danish *Papirer* are given in terms of volume, part, section, and entry. References to the English *Journals* are to the entry rather than to the page, unless the page is explicitly given.

Notes to the Prayers

1. Thy Greatness, My Nothingness: *Journals*, 278.
2. Thine Is the Power: *Papirer*, VII, A, 380.
3. Thou Art Incomprehensible: *ibid.*, VII, A, 142.
4. Thou Art Unchangeable: *For Self-Examination*, p. 227.
5. Thy Word: *ibid.*, p. 39.
6. Thou God of Love: *Works of Love*, p. 4.
7. O Infinite Love: *Papirer*, X^3, A, 49.
8. Thou Hast Loved Us First: *ibid.*, IV, B, 171.
9. Thou Who Hast First Loved Us: *ibid.*, X^3, A, 421.
10. Thou Hearest Our Cry: *ibid.*, VII, A, 132.
11. Thy Loving Care: *ibid.*, X^1, A, 633.
12. Thy Fatherly Care: *ibid.*, X^2, A, 342.
13. Have Then a Little Patience: *ibid.*, VIII, A, 255.
14. Let Us Not Forget: *ibid.*, II, A, 309.
15. Hold Not Our Sins: *Journals*, 692.
16. Seeking Thee in the Confession of Sins: From Kierkegaard's *Thoughts on Crucial Situations in Human Life*, p. 2, translated by David F. Swenson, copyright 1941, Augsburg Publishing House, Minneapolis, Minn. Used by permission.
17. Against You Have I Sinned: *Journals*, 1360.
18. Thou Art Able To Heal: *Sickness unto Death*, pp. x-xi.

19. Give Us Also a Sign: *Journals*, 257.

20. The Supreme Danger: *Papirer*, VIII, A, 367.

21. Thy Forgiveness: *ibid.*, IX, A, 328.

22. We Belong to Thee: *ibid.*, III, C, 1.

23. To Will One Thing: *Purity of Heart*, pp. 31-32.

24. That I May Believe: From Kierkegaard's *Edifying Discourses*, III, 120, translated by David F. and Lillian Marvin Swenson, copyright 1945, Augsburg Publishing House, Minneapolis, Minn. Used by permission.

25. Committed to Thee: From Kierkegaard's *Edifying Discourses*, I, 33, translated by David F. and Lillian Marvin Swenson, copyright 1943, Augsburg Publishing House, Minneapolis, Minn. Used by permission.

26. That We May Be Faithful: *Papirer*, X³, A, 108.

27. For Faith: *ibid.*, X, A, 632.

28. To Know Thy Will: *ibid.*, II, A, 313.

29. At Thy Command: *Journals*, 254.

30. Not Like Strangers: *Papirer*, II, A, 377.

31. For Courage: *Journals*, 350.

32. Let Me Not Be Discouraged: *Papirer*, VII, A, 136.

33. For Thy Peace: *ibid.*, II, A, 318.

34. For Peace and Assurance: *Journals*, 330.

35. From the Lilies and the Birds Let Us Learn: *Christian Discourses*, p. 11.

36. That We Might Learn: *ibid.*, p. 315.

37. Guides for the Troubled: From Kierkegaard's *The Gospel of Suffering*, p. 168, translated by David F. Swenson and Lillian Marvin Swenson, copyright 1948, Augsburg Publishing House, Minneapolis, Minn. Used by permission.

38. The Thought of Thee: *Journals*, 248.

39. I Will Continue To Pray: *Papirer*, III, A, 158.

40. Help Us To Pray: *ibid.*, II, A, 308.

41. Love of Thee Maketh Eloquent: *ibid.*, III, A, 162.
42. For Self-mastery: *ibid.*, II, A, 334.
43. Be Near to Us: *ibid.*, II, A, 295.
44. We Would Turn toward Thee: *ibid.*, VI, B, 164.
45. We Seek Thee at This Hour: *ibid.*, II, A, 285.
46. Our Dependence on Thee: *ibid.*, II, A, 327.
47. Draw Near to Me, O God: *Journals*, 310.
48. Let Us Feel Thy Presence: *Papirer*, X, A, 210.
49. Thou Art Near: *Journals*, 604.
50. Thy Love Is beyond All Proof: *Papirer*, X^3, A, 223.
51. A Goodness Greater than the Human Heart Can Understand: From Kierkegaard's *Edifying Discourses*, I, 92, translated by David F. and Lillian Marvin Swenson, copyright 1943, Augsburg Publishing House, Minneapolis, Minn. Used by permission.
52. Every Good and Perfect Gift: *ibid.*, p. 55.
53. All Things Work Together for Good to Them That Love Thee: *Papirer*, X^3, A, 222.
54. Whatever Comes of Thee: *ibid.*, X^4, A, 229.
55. We Would Receive All: *ibid.*, X, A, 470.
56. Not Empty Handed: *ibid.*, IV, B, 175.
57. Every Creature Turns Its Eyes to Thee: *ibid.*, III, A, 86.
58. It Is from Thy Hand: *ibid.*, II, A, 554.
59. All Things Come of Thee: *ibid.*, VIII, A, 342.
60. Give Us Strength: *ibid.*, III, A, 32.
61. Thine Infinite Wisdom: *ibid.*, X^3, A, 595.
62. One Thing Will Remain: *ibid.*, X^3, A, 291.
63. Thou Dost Not Love Me for My Merits: *ibid.*, X^3, A, 227.
64. Thy Silence: *ibid.*, VII, A, 131.
65. The Joy in Suffering: *ibid.*, X^4, A, 488.
66. Keep Me from Becoming a Fool: *ibid.*, VII, A, 133.
67. Thanks Be to God: *Journals*, 210.

68. Whither Should We Turn? *Christian Discourses*, p. 361.

69. To Whom Can We Turn? *For Self-Examination*, p. 9.

70. Thou Art Our Only Hiding Place: *ibid.*, p. 18.

71. Draw Us to Thee: *Training in Christianity*, p. 251.

72. There Is So Much To Drag Us Back: *ibid.*, p. 151.

73. Weak Is Our Foolish Heart: *ibid.*, p. 157.

74. Unto Thee in Lowliness: *ibid.*, p. 167.

75. Thy Life Is the Judgment: *ibid.*, p. 180.

76. Thou Art the Strongest: *Papirer*, VIII, A, 372.

77. Help Us To Love Thee: *Christian Discourses*, p. 379.

78. Thou Alone Art Able: *Papirer*, IX, A, 120.

79. Suffering: *ibid.*, X^6, B, 239.

80. A Whole Life Long: *Journals*, 1030.

81. Not To Admire but To Follow: *Training in Christianity*, p. 227.

82. Would That We Might Follow Thee: *For Self-Examination*, p. 77.

83. Pattern and Redeemer: *ibid.*, p. 161.

84. Thine Example: From Kierkegaard's *Gospel of Suffering*, p. 4, translated by David F. Swenson and Lillian Marvin Swenson, copyright 1948, Augsburg Publishing House, Minneapolis, Minn. Used by permission.

85. Help Me To Think of Thee: *Papirer*, X^3, A, 11.

86. Thy Church Militant: *Training in Christianity*, p. 197.

87. Enlighten Our Minds: *Christian Discourses*, p. 371.

88. Thou Spirit of Holiness: *Papirer*, X^2, A, 344.

89. Bless This Our Gathering: *For Self-Examination*, p. 93.

90. Send Therefore Thy Spirit: *ibid.*, p. 113.

91. O Holy Spirit: *ibid.*, p. 106.

92. The New Year: From Kierkegaard's *Edifying Discourses*, I, 6, translated by David F. and Lillian Marvin Swenson, copy-

right 1943, Augsburg Publishing House, Minneapolis, Minn.
Used by permission.

93. At the Lord's Table: *Christian Discourses*, p. 259.
94. At the Lord's Table: *ibid.*, p. 269.
95. At the Lord's Table: *ibid.*, pp. 275-76.
96. At the Lord's Table: *ibid.*, pp. 283-84.
97. At the Lord's Table: *ibid.*, p. 289.
98. At the Lord's Table: *ibid.*, p. 297.
99. At the Lord's Table: *ibid.*, p. 305.

Notes to Chapter 1

* Kierkegaard's authorship is a complex phenomenon. A concise survey of the major works may be found in the Swensons' introduction to Volume II of their translation of the *Edifying Discourses*. In summary, however, his published works may be divided, as he divided them, into the aesthetic and the religious. The aesthetic works, which themselves had a hidden and indirect religious motivation, were written during the period 1843-1846. They include *Either/Or* (1843), *Repetition* (1843), *Fear and Trembling* (1843), *Philosophical Fragments* (1844), *The Concept of Dread* (1844), *Stages on Life's Way* (1845), and the *Concluding Unscientific Postscript* (1846). The religious works paralleled the aesthetic from the beginning; they were written under Kierkegaard's own name, whereas the aesthetic works were published pseudonymously. Nine *Edifying Discourses* were published in 1843 and nine in 1844. Though these works were signed by Kierkegaard, they were written from the point of view of religious immanence. Three more discourses "on imagined occasions," published in English under the title, *Thoughts on Crucial Situations in Human Life*, were issued in 1845. These discourses move beyond the perspective of religious immanence and intro-

duce the period of Kierkegaard's religious authorship in a narrower sense. During the year 1847 Kierkegaard published *Works of Love* and three edifying discourses "in various spirits," *Purity of Heart, The Gospel of Suffering,* and *The Lilies of the Field.* The latter two discourses have been issued in English under the title, *The Gospel of Suffering. Christian Discourses* followed in the next year, and though *The Point of View of My Work as an Author* was written during the same period, it was not published until 1859 after Kierkegaard's death. Kierkegaard's last major works were *Sickness unto Death* (1849), *Training in Christianity* (1850), and *For Self-Examination* (1851). *Judge for Yourselves* was written in 1851-52 but not published until 1876. In 1854-55 Kierkegaard published numerous polemical articles which have been collected and translated into English under the title, *Attack on Christendom.* A number of shorter essays, discourses, and sermons not mentioned in this summary were published during the years of Kierkegaard's literary productivity. *The Book on Adler,* written and rewritten in 1846-47, was not published during Kierkegaard's lifetime. It has, however, recently been made available in English under the title, *On Authority and Revelation, The Book on Adler.*

1. *Journals*, 431.
2. *Point of View*, p. 76.
3. *Journals*, p. 560.
4. *Postscript*, p. 551.
5. M. Heidegger, *Sein und Zeit*, p. 235 n. cited by M. Wyschogrod in *Kierkegaard and Heidegger* (New York: Humanities Press, 1954).
6. *Journals*, 16.
7. *Ibid.*, 22.
8. *Ibid.*
9. *Ibid.*, 4, 16, 20, 222, 335, 784.

10. *Ibid.*, 22.
11. *Ibid.*, 773.
12. *Ibid.*, 27.
13. *Ibid.*, 32.
14. *Ibid.*, 51.
15. *Ibid.*, 88.
16. *Ibid.*, 174.
17. *Ibid.*, 196.
18. *Ibid.*, 211.
19. *Ibid.*, 337.
20. *Point of View*, p. 73.
21. *Ibid.*, p. 154.
22. *Journals*, 194, 465.
23. *Ibid.*, 425.
24. *Ibid.*, 432.
25. *Ibid.*, 638.
26. *Ibid.*, 660, 704.
27. *Ibid.*, 734.
28. *Ibid.*, 735.
29. *Ibid.*, 1192.
30. *Ibid.*, 1401.
31. *Ibid.*, 644.
32. *Ibid.*, 645.
33. *Ibid.*, 861.
34. *Ibid.*, 694.
35. *Ibid.*, 1220.
36. *Ibid.*, 905.
37. *Ibid.*, 936.
38. *Ibid.*, 970.
39. *Ibid.*, 1114.
40. *Ibid.*, 763.
41. *Ibid.*, 1225.

42. Cf. *ibid.*, 600, 681.

43. *Ibid.*, 775.

44. *Training in Christianity*, pp. 175-78.

45. *Journals*, 207.

46. *Ibid.*, 600.

47. *Ibid.*, 903.

48. Johannes Hohlenberg, *Soren Kierkegaard* (New York: Pantheon Books, Inc., 1954), p. 167.

49. *Journals*, 747.

50. *Ibid.*, 748.

51. *Ibid.*, 749.

52. *Ibid.*, 763.

53. *Ibid.*, 754.

Notes to Chapter 2

1. *Either/Or*, II, 151.

2. *Purity of Heart*, cf. pp. 53-67.

3. *Either/Or*, II, 21.

4. *Ibid.*, p. 149.

5. *Postscript*, p. 265.

6. *Either/Or*, II, 141.

7. *Ibid.*, p. 152.

8. *Ibid.*, p. 193.

9. *Ibid.*, p. 142.

10. *Ibid.*, p. 189.

11. *Ibid.*, p. 150.

12. *Ibid.*, pp. 153-54.

13. *Ibid.*, p. 165.

14. *Ibid.*, p. 162.

15. *Ibid.*, p. 153.

16. *Point of View*, p. 42.

17. *Postscript*, p. 295.

18. *Ibid.*, p. 274.
19. David Swenson, *Something about Kierkegaard* (Minneapolis: Augsburg Publishing House, 1945), p. 143.
20. *Postscript*, pp. 70, 85.
21. *Ibid.*, p. 133.
22. *Ibid.*, p. 88.
23. *Ibid.*, pp. 270-71.
24. *Ibid.*, p. 90.
25. *Ibid.*, p. 107.
26. *Ibid.*, p. 279.
27. *Ibid.*, p. 70.
28. *Ibid.*, pp. 307, 315, also *Journals*, 1050.
29. *Postscript*, p. 276.
30. *Concept of Dread*, pp. 9, 12.
31. *Postscript*, p. 272.
32. *Ibid.*, p. 99.
33. *Ibid.*, p. 74.
34. *Ibid.*, p. 272 n.
35. *Ibid.*, p. 266.
36. *Ibid.*, p. 506.
37. *Ibid.*
38. *Fragments*, p. 59.
39. *Postscript*, pp. 324-26.
40. *Ibid.*, p. 339.
41. *Ibid.*, p. 43.
42. *Training in Christianity*, p. 139.

Notes to Chapter 3

1. *Journals*, 1158.
2. Cf. *Postscript*, p. 230.
3. *Either/Or*, II, 162.

4. Swenson, *Something about Kierkegaard* (Minneapolis: Augsburg Publishing House, 1945), p. 34.

5. *Either/Or*, II, 179.

6. *Works of Love*, p. 34.

7. *Ibid.*, pp. 203 ff.

8. *Sickness unto Death*, p. 111.

9. *Ibid.*, p. 129.

10. *Ibid.*, p. 154.

11. *Thoughts on Crucial Situations*, pp. 47-48.

12. *Concept of Dread*, p. 39.

13. *Journals*, 1177.

14. *Concept of Dread*, p. 85.

15. *Sickness unto Death*, p. 17.

16. Swenson, *op. cit.*, and E. E. Smith, "Psychological Aspects of Kierkegaard," *Character and Personality*, XII (1943), 195-206.

17. *Either/Or*, II, 217.

18. *Sickness unto Death*, p. 43.

19. Swenson, *op. cit.*, p. 51.

20. *Sickness unto Death*, p. 44.

21. *Either/Or*, II, 180.

22. *Ibid.*, p. 187.

23. *Postscript*, p. 239.

24. *Point of View*, p. 121; also *Journals*, 614.

25. *Journals*, 632.

26. *Point of View*, p. 130.

27. *Postscript*, p. 240.

28. *Ibid.*, p. 364.

29. *Ibid.*, p. 387.

30. *Ibid.*, p. 388.

31. *Ibid.*, p. 472.

32. *Training in Christianity*, p. 155.

33. *Concept of Dread*, p. 46.

34. *Journals*, 967.
35. *Concept of Dread*, p. 38.
36. *Ibid.*, p. 55.
37. *Ibid.*, p. 47.
38. *Ibid.*, p. 139.
39. *Ibid.*, p. 141.
40. *Ibid.*, p. 142.
41. *Ibid.*
42. *Ibid.*, p. 140.
43. *Ibid.*
44. *Ibid.*, p. 104.
45. *Sickness unto Death*, p. 156.
46. *Postscript*, p. 209.
47. *Concept of Dread*, p. 142.
48. *Repetition*, p. 144.
49. *Ibid.*, pp. 3, 33.
50. W. Lowrie, *Kierkegaard* (London: Oxford University Press, 1938), p. 630.
51. *Postscript*, p. 53.
52. *Training in Christianity*, p. 220.
53. *Postscript*, p. 33.
54. *Ibid.*, p. 277.
55. *Ibid.*, p. 353.
56. Swenson, *op. cit.*, p. 144.
57. *Concept of Dread*, p. 99.
58. *Works of Love*, p. 193.

Notes to Chapter 4

1. *Papirer*, VIII¹, A, 532.
2. *Ibid.*, IX, A, 316.
3. *Ibid.*, 462.
4. *Journals*, 894.

5. *Edifying Discourses*, IV, 113 ff.
6. *Journals*, 774.
7. *Ibid.*, 118.
8. *Ibid.*, 119.
9. *Ibid.*, 173.
10. *Ibid.*, 238.
11. *Ibid.*, 369.
12. *Ibid.*, 388.
13. *Ibid.*, 350.
14. *Ibid.*, 588.
15. *Ibid.*
16. *Ibid.*, 627.
17. *Ibid.*, 1031.
18. *Ibid.*, 1220.
19. *Ibid.*
20. *Ibid.*, 815.
21. *Ibid.*, 1047.
22. *Papirer*, IX, A, 65.
23. *Journals*, 754.
24. *Papirer*, IX, A, 65.
25. *Journals*, 335.
26. *Ibid.*, 754.
27. *Ibid.*, 1252.
28. K. Jaspers, "The Importance of Kierkegaard," *Cross Currents*, II, No. 3 (Spring, 1952), 5-16.
29. *Journals*, 1287.
30. *Papirer*, X^5, A, 81.
31. *Ibid.*, X^3, A, 531.
32. *Purity of Heart*, p. 55.
33. *Papirer*, IX, A, 316; X^2, A, 76.
34. *Ibid.*
35. *Ibid.*, X^4, A, 281.

36. *Ibid.*, X¹, A, 64; IX, A, 316.

37. *Ibid.*, X², A, 644; III, A, 126; IX, A, 24.

38. *Ibid.*, VII¹, A, 28.

39. *Ibid.*, XI¹, A, 95.

40. *Christian Discourses*, p. 67.

41. *Ibid.*, p. 306.

42. *Edifying Discourses*, IV, 113 ff.

43. *Journals*, 1282.

44. From Kierkegaard's *Edifying Discourses*, IV, 142, translated by David F. and Lillian Marvin Swenson, copyright 1946, Augsburg Publishing House, Minneapolis, Minn. Used by permission.

45. *Christian Discourses*, p. 271; also *Papirer*, X³, A, 317.

46. *Papirer*, X², A, 197.

47. *Purity of Heart*, p. 182.

48. *Christian Discourses*, pp. 176-77.

49. *Papirer*, X³, A, 317.

50. *Journals*, 974.

51. *Christian Discourses*, p. 25.

52. *Ibid.*, p. 330.

53. *Ibid.*, p. 323.

54. *Journals*, 572.

55. *Christian Discourses*, p. 324.

56. *Papirer*, II, A, 537; IV, A, 145; IV, A, 171.

57. *Purity of Heart*, p. 51.

58. *Papirer*, II, A, 537.

59. *Journals*, 617.

60. *Christian Discourses*, p. 295.

61. *Papirer*, X⁴, A, 297.

62. *Ibid.*

63. *Edifying Discourses*, I, No. 2, No. 5 *passim; Christian Discourses*, pp. 57 f.; *Papirer*, VIII¹, A, 253.

64. *Papirer*, X², A, 644; X⁵, A, 81; X⁵, A, 79; X², A, 348.
65. *Journals*, 1262.
66. *Papirer*, X⁴, A, 565.
67. *Journals*, 1270, 1287.
68. *Papirer*, X⁵, A, 81.
69. *Ibid.*, X³, A, 747.
70. *Ibid.*, XI¹, A, 382.
71. *Christian Discourses*, pp. 20, 109.
72. *Ibid.*, pp. 354-55.
73. *Papirer*, VIII¹, A, 302.
74. *Christian Discourses*, pp. 18-19.
75. *Thoughts on Crucial Situations*, p. 5.
76. *Journals*, 784.
77. *Ibid.*, 287.
78. *Papirer*, VIII¹, A, 77.
79. *Ibid.*, X⁵, A, 51.
80. *Ibid.*, X⁵, A, 52.
81. *Ibid.*, X², A, 595.
82. *Ibid.*, II, A, 301.
83. *Journals*, p. 550.

The Works of Kierkegaard

THE WORKS OF KIERKEGAARD
IN ENGLISH

Attack upon "Christendom." Translated by WALTER LOWRIE. Princeton: Princeton University Press, 1944.

On Authority and Revelation, The Book on Adler. Translated with an introduction and notes by WALTER LOWRIE. Princeton: Princeton University Press, 1955.

Christian Discourses. Translated by WALTER LOWRIE. London: Oxford University Press, 1940.

The Concept of Dread. Translated by WALTER LOWRIE. Princeton: Princeton University Press, 1944.

Concluding Unscientific Postscript to the "Philosophical Fragments." Translated by DAVID F. SWENSON; completed and edited by WALTER LOWRIE. Princeton: Princeton University Press, 1941.

Edifying Discourses. 4 vols. Translated by DAVID F. and LILLIAN MARVIN SWENSON. Minneapolis: Augsburg Publishing House, 1943–46.

Either/Or: A Fragment of Life. Volume I translated by DAVID F. and LILLIAN MARVIN SWENSON; Volume II translated by WALTER LOWRIE. Princeton: Princeton University Press, 1944.

Fear and Trembling. Translated by WALTER LOWRIE. Princeton: Princeton University Press, 1941.

The Gospel of Suffering. Translated by DAVID F. and LILLIAN MARVIN SWENSON. Minneapolis: Augsburg Publishing House, 1948.

The Journals of Soren Kierkegaard. A selection edited and translated by ALEXANDER DRU. London: Oxford University Press, 1938.

The Lilies and the Birds. Translated by A. S. ALDWORTH and W. S. FERRIE. London: Daniel, 1941.

Philosophical Fragments. Translated and with an introduction by DAVID F. SWENSON. Princeton: Princeton University Press, 1944.

The Point of View for My Work as an Author. Translated by WALTER LOWRIE. London: Oxford University Press, 1939.

The Present Age. Translated by ALEXANDER DRU and WALTER LOWRIE. London: Oxford University Press, 1940.

Purity of Heart Is To Will One Thing. Rev. ed. Translated by DOUGLAS V. STEERE. New York: Harper & Bros., 1948.

Repetition. Translated by WALTER LOWRIE. Princeton: Princeton University Press, 1941.

For Self-Examination and *Judge for Yourselves!* Translated by WALTER LOWRIE (except the final discourse, "God's Unchangeableness," translated by DAVID F. SWENSON). Princeton: Princeton University Press, 1944.

The Sickness unto Death. Translated by WALTER LOWRIE. Princeton: Princeton University Press, 1941.

Stages on Life's Way. Translated by WALTER LOWRIE. Princeton: Princeton University Press, 1940.

Thoughts on Crucial Situations in Human Life: Three Discourses on Imagined Occasions. Translated by DAVID F. SWENSON. Minneapolis: Augsburg Publishing House, 1941.

Training in Christianity. Translated by WALTER LOWRIE. Princeton: Princeton University Press, 1944.

Works of Love. Translated by DAVID F. and LILLIAN MARVIN SWENSON. Princeton: Princeton University Press, 1946.

Citations to *Papirer* are to the Danish edition of *Soren Kierkegaards Papirer*, edited by P. A. HEIBERG, V. KUHR, and E. TORSTING. 11 vols. Copenhagen: Gyldendalske Boghandel Nordisk Forlag, 1909-48.

SIGNIFICANT WORKS DEALING WITH SOREN KIERKEGAARD'S
LIFE AND THOUGHT

COLLINS, J. *The Mind of Kierkegaard.* Chicago: Henry Regnery Co., 1953.

CROXALL, T. H. *Kierkegaard Studies.* London: Lutterworth Press, 1948.

GEISMAR, E. *Lectures on the Religious Thought of Soren Kierkegaard.* Minneapolis: Augsburg Publishing House, 1937.

HIRSCH, E. *Kierkegaard-Studien.* 2 vols. Gütersloh: C. Bertelsmann, 1933.

HOHLENBERG, J. *Soren Kierkegaard.* New York: Pantheon Books, Inc., 1954.

LOWRIE, W. *Kierkegaard.* London: Oxford University Press, 1938.

SWENSON, D. *Something about Kierkegaard.* Rev. ed. Minneapolis: Augsburg Publishing House, 1945.

THOMTE, R. *Kierkegaard's Philosophy of Religion.* Princeton: Princeton University Press, 1948.

WAHL, J. *Etudes Kierkegaardiennes.* 2d ed. Paris: J. Vrin, 1949.